The Future of the Skyscraper

Philip Nobel
Bruce Sterling
Tom Van...
Matthew
Diana Lin...
Will Self
Emily Badger
Dickson Despommier
Michael Govan

SOM Thinkers

Philip Nobel is an architecture critic and architect.

Bruce Sterling is a science fiction writer, Internet critic, and cyberspace theorist.

Tom Vanderbilt is a journalist, blogger, and visiting scholar at NYU's Rudin Center for Transportation Policy and Management.

Matthew Yglesias is the Executive Editor of Vox media.

Diana Lind is the Director of Digital Audience Development for the Philadelphia Media Network.

Will Self is a writer, journalist, and television commentator.

Emily Badger writes on national urban policy for *The Washington Post*.

Dickson Despommier is a professor in the Department of Environmental Health Sciences at Columbia University's Mailman School of Public Health.

Michael Govan is the Director of the Los Angeles County Museum of Art (LACMA).

10 07471582

SOM Partners' Foreword

From its inception, SOM has practiced architecture as part of a public trust. We have always understood that architecture exists within a complex system of cultural dependencies, and that it is only through understanding that complexity that fitting and inspiring designs can come to exist. Buildings comprise a society's hopes, solve its problems, project its values, and become physical markers of the approach to our highest ideals.

That essential work can never be successful if it is conducted in isolation. Throughout our history, we have endeavored to join the practice of architecture with the practice of good citizenship—through responsible engagement with the cities where we build, through the implementation of progressive technologies, through the forward-looking research conducted under the auspices of SOM, the SOM Foundation, CASE, and the SOM Journal. The book you hold in your hands is an extension of that critical tradition.

The subject here is one that is integral to who we are. We consider the ongoing stewardship of progress in the design of tall buildings to be an essential strain of the firm's DNA. But when we turned our minds to considering the future of this rapidly developing building type—what comes next?—we knew we needed, once again, to engage the question from the widest perspective: a public perspective. It is our hope that this book, a collection of the thoughts of expert writers considering the future of the skyscraper within their own broad spheres of expertise, will inspire even broader discussions—a collective conversation about the future of our shared environment that we all must join.

Introduction:
The Future of the Skyscraper

Philip Nobel

One hundred and sixty-three floors; 2,723 feet to the top of the spire. For a moment, and by a solid 745-foot margin, the tallest building in the world.

The Burj Khalifa's statistics are well-known, numbers meant to impress us with their novelty, stand-ins for exceptional experience. But is it really something new, reaching farther into the sky? Is it truly a different world up there, so high above the terrestrial norm, gazing down on passing weather, or, on a clear day, as residents report, looking straight across the Persian Gulf to the distant shores of Iran?

When it was first occupied, half a decade ago, news organizations dutifully interviewed tenants and owners, or invited some of the domestic aeronauts themselves to write their own reports. The results were universally and uniformly bland. Paeans to world-class service. Shout-outs to awesome views. Confronted by a technological product that encroaches on the sublime, even those closest to it could do little more than fall back on the mundane terminology of real estate. "There is an indoor and outdoor pool, a yoga room, a massage room, and gym for each set of floors," an owner of several Burj apartments told a reporter. Only in one story, a first-person account prepared for *The New York Times* by an American couple living on the 98th floor, did we get a hint of something more: "This is a building that calls us…to be grand in our own aspirations, just as the building is itself."

Grand in aspiration. Familiar in result. So what's new at the bleeding edge of building tall? There is an incessant drive for height recorded in the history of architecture—a universal drive, as evident in Dubai as elsewhere today, that is not reducible to economic impulse alone. The tight grids and real estate constraints of Chicago and Manhattan gave us the

earliest true skyscrapers, and a story to go with
them that was less true but pleasing to modern minds
looking for a rational justification for form. Ever-
increasing height, we were taught, was but a direct,
one-to-one effect of resource scarcity—too little land
to satisfy too great a demand. Skyscrapers, however
lofty and inspiring, were merely machines to multiply
the value of their sites.

And yet there is a lot of room in Dubai. Set amid
so much emptiness, on the very edge of untouched
wilderness, no one can argue that it had to go
so high to redeem an initial investment in a particular interchangeable bit of unbound desert. Our
new very-tall towers carry with them that familiar
twentieth-century mythos, and the timeless language
of the mercantile, even as they are made possible
by means and methods that are decidedly twenty-first.
Still, though they embody a complexity as cultural
products that is shared by all architecture—at once an
index of the social, political, material, economic,
natural, aesthetic, and even emotional forces acting
on a given chunk of land—the new supertalls, as
they have come to be known, demand consideration
beyond other classes of buildings. We need to reconsider the standard fables about what dictates their
rising: though perhaps an argument could be made
for accretive value, net gain by a city or a state, it's
not really about money.

Instead, this new cohort of superlative-straining
towers makes plain an ancient emotional impetus
that was a skyward pressure, too, on previous generations of tall buildings. Not dollars and cents. Not
spreadsheets and leases and codes. Certainly not the
litany of features through which an agent might sell
of a piece of property in the sky. No, there's something else driving the height race. Something primal,

competitive, romantic, eternal: some consequence of human minds, hard-wired to love a prospect, a mountain, needing to be high to feel safe from threat, congenitally driven to manufacture a marker on the land—the higher the better, and better still if it can be the highest of them all.

Seen as they are, symptoms of a psychological need, skyscrapers are at once exceptional and deeply normative. Stunning and plain. In a word not often applied to assemblies of concrete, steel and cold glass, they can be seen to be deeply and essentially human.

Still, hobbled by decades of false economic justification, we lack the language now, the tropes, the theory, the mythology to assimilate our new skyscrapers; too much coverage is but some slightly elevated version of an observer raising eyes to a distant pinnacle, extending a shaking finger, rattling off empty statistics meant to awe.

Rallying adjectives to the cause is no better. To truly understand on their own terms, the ancient terms, the many Khalifa-class projects now under construction—buildings such as Jeddah's Kingdom Tower (designed for 3,281 feet, or a clean kilometer), Suzhou's Zhongnan Center (2,392 feet), and Shenzhen's Ping An Finance Center (2,165), or the next super- or megatall coming not-at-all-figuratively over the horizon—we need to adapt our cultural rules to locate the experience of great height, as the residents of the Burj attempted, in a place that is of, not alien to, daily life. To date, these buildings have been well accommodated by the global economic-development and engineering practices that beget them. The technical jargon has long been in place to define and describe them, resources at the ready to go yet higher. But before we do, it may be wise to truly

know what we have. Supertalls must be accessioned
into story. Into action and image. Into culture.

Over the last few years, that important work has
in part fallen (I use the word advisedly here) to an
international cadre of daredevil adventurers. As
Philippe Petit did for the Twin Towers of the World
Trade Center when he stepped out between them
1,300-odd feet over the hard lower Manhattan
ground, his spiritual descendants today are putting
their bodies on the line to act as vectors for our
fears and dreams. Humanizing vectors—a troupe of
young Russians, popularizing its illicit feats through
the deft manipulation of social media, has made
images of supertall spire-stands and cornice-hangs
as much a part of the story of those buildings as
the architects' own cloud-piercing sunset renderings.
Another gang of young aerialists made a fuss
by breaking into and climbing The Shard before its
completion—an essential episode in London's long,
noisy path to an understanding of that intrusive
object's place in its civic self-regard. Well before its
opening, Manhattan's One World Trade had several
encounters with this sort of guerrilla culture-work.
First when a team of B.A.S.E. jumpers took a short,
spiraling parachute fall down from the top (recorded
by GoPro and eventually shared on YouTube), and
later when a New Jersey teenager crawled through
a fence and strolled to the top to snap selfies (he
was caught, given community service, and arrested
again months later while climbing a water tower
in Weehawken—undone by that undeniable human
urge for heights). Those two modes of incursion, the
latter lackadaisical, the former mad, were, before the
building was occupied and the observation deck was
open, the only means available at the time to bodily

claim Manhattan's highest point; lacking a twin, there is no place to stretch a rope.

Though it can hardly be encouraged—given the history of the site, the World Trade Center breaches were particularly high-risk—such acts of derring-do begin to signal a communal importance for these structures that goes well beyond the conventional mode in which they are inhabited or the manner in which they are typically celebrated from afar. Engines of industry, expressions of ego or will, tall towers are nonetheless, when they pierce the shared skies, intensely public. Without a stretch, they can be seen as works of a type—acting on ageless psychology, straining comprehension—that can be understood as public art. We can ask of them, then, artistic questions: What do we make of these things we make? What do they mean? But also, because architecture is forever tied by its own limitations to the limitless matrix of real life, we can ask of them questions of a political, economic and technological nature—as well as those questions, at once more universal and more intimate, that touch on the body and the mind and the soul. How grand are your aspirations?

Questions are at the center of this book, what is intended to be the first in a series that aims to look beyond the field of architecture and its familiar cadres to solicit the thoughts and opinions of those outside what is all-too-often an isolated subculture. Other volumes will address other types of buildings, or works of infrastructure, or urban settings. But they will employ a similar method to get at their respective "futures." The writing here is not oracular but practical—not false certainties but true takes— by observers free of the assumptions made by those directly involved in conceiving and realizing the spaces in which we live. Architecture, even as it sprawls between the domains of art and mind, technology and financial power, touching all the hot buttons and levers in each, has had, historically, a tendency to turn inward, to self-analysis rather than frank exploration when it faces big issues of cultural churn and change. This is not always a responsible strategy for a profession charged with no less than the construction of the arenas of life in an interdependent and increasingly trans-disciplinary world, and it is a great credit to SOM, in initiating and sponsoring this project, to have recognized that fact.

Here, then, we look forward, together–taking as a given that the close examination of past and present is essential not only to understanding, but to determining, the future. So we have Bruce Sterling, pioneering cyberpunk novelist and critic of technology, describing some possible futures that might shape future towers. His essay also serves as a primer on (or a master class in) how to think like a futurist–a responsible futurist in the contemporary mode, wary of the futurism of the last century and before, that, in its drive to transcend the present, might verge close to fantasy. He presents a choose-your-own-adventure of politically- and economically-aware cultural possibilities for architecture, some of them terrifying in their nearness.

That will be useful training as we peer up at skyscrapers old and new, visit their highest floors, turn them this way and that to see them clear. Through the psychology (Tom Vanderbilt) and physiology (Emily Badger) of living and working on high. Through the lens of policy–politics and law–in the low-rise counterexample of Washington, D.C. (Matthew Yglesias). Diana Lind tests the idea of tall against the expressed needs, more ground-hugging, of those spatially mundane but transformative new economy industries that may be the supertall clients of the future (but, perhaps tellingly, now are not). Will Self looks back to write forward toward a new understanding of the tower in the popular imagination—the themes and memes and dreads and dreams that, however much we wish to imagine ourselves in new cultural spaces, we only shake with great difficulty. But shake them we must: because the planet is imperiled, because consensus is forming that increased urban density may be one way to limit that peril, and, in much of the urbanized world, building more, and smarter, does still mean building high. Michael Govan offers up the artist Yuri Avvakumov and his plaintive House of Cards series as a way to see past the architecture of towers, perhaps more clearly, to the emotional forces that, in the final analysis, they must always address. To close the collection, we look beyond the tall building altogether. Dickson Despommier, the father of the vertical farm, shares here a comprehensive vision of an ecological future: one in which land is managed responsibly inspired by the genius of nature; one in which cities consolidate so that nature may be relieved of human pressures entirely; and one in which towers, perhaps supertall towers, would necessarily play a crucial role.

A final note on height. The Chicago-based Council on Tall Buildings and Urban Habitat has become the authority, the Oxford English and Guinness Book in one. It defines as "supertall" any tower that surpasses 300 meters (984 feet); as this is written, there are seventy-three examples scattered around the world, from the Capital City Tower in Moscow (990 feet) to the now-venerable Taipei 101 (1,667), once, now quaintly, the tallest building in the world. Anything higher than 600 meters (1,968 feet) is, per the CTBUH, "megatall." To date, the Burj

Khalifa and the Makkah Royal Clock Tower Hotel
in Mecca are built; nine others are under construction
or seriously proposed. It's a comforting, scientistic
way to parse the numbers. Yet, as in all efforts to
categorize human endeavor, something essential is
lost in the categories. Perhaps in time we'll get
to a point where data flows so free and so true that
engineers will be able to model fear and desire
and confusion and joy, combine those forces parametrically and pull the product of their equations
up into a cloud-piercing spire. Perhaps in time it will
become true that towers are really only about
the bottom line. But until then, it will fall to architecture to creatively and responsibly manage those
qualities of the human mind, and to observers of
architecture, such as those writing here, to question it.

The Unbuilt Towers
of Futurity

Bruce Sterling

Some among my readers may recall a dreadful incident, created by a dark genius of political theater, in September of 2001. This dismal act involved aircraft and skyscrapers. It so transfixed the public imagination that some feared skyscrapers would no longer be built.

Over a dozen years later, and we can see: quite the opposite came to pass. Skyscrapers multiplied in many locales never before graced with their presence. They showed impressive formal vitality, in a startling panoply of unheard-of shapes and stylings.

Today's supertall structures, seen objectively, are risky, daring, even rather scary. Yet they inspire no apparent fear; the public greets them with kindness and complacency.

There are some complaints, of course, those standard complaints: the aggressive, thrusting showiness, the lack of a straightforward business model, the spoilt views of historic skylines. Identical things were said about the Eiffel Tower in the 1880s.

Old-fashioned complaints rarely pose big problems for innovators. Technologies in real trouble with society—nuclear power, for instance—are continually generating new, exciting complaints. Skyscrapers, even the tallest ones, are becoming urbane.

The newer ones have looser floor-plans, a wider variety of uses and users; more cozy creature comforts, less of the boxy, steel-framed swaying and creaking. In short, they're a modern case study in good old-fashioned technological advance. Novelty abounds in skyscraperdom today. New design methods, stronger materials, advances in building management, exotic fabrication methods, political smart-city initiatives—these promise a host of surprises.

So this is a fun time for skyscraper speculations. I may mention that, as I write, I just got through with a lively project for Arizona State University, involving a tower over ten miles high. This would seem to be the tallest possible structure that is buildable with today's methods and materials. This notion has been a pleasant locus for some Arthur C. Clarke-style aerospace engineering by us sci-fi writers. I can't help but tell you that this imaginary edifice would weigh twelve million tons, and it would likely have to be extruded upward from the planet's surface, from some desert test-bed....But never mind: that's all science fiction.

Today's supertalls may boggle the mind, but they are stunningly factual, immediately obvious, impossible to overlook. It's their children, the unbuilt towers of futurity, that are surrounded by a dense, foggy haze of harbingers. Futurist scenarios can prove useful here. Scenarios cause loose ideas to separate and clump into trends.

I'll do a little quadrant-work in my brief essay here, and describe four differing yet plausible classes of future skyscraper. Let's choose a twenty year time-frame: the 2030s.

Let's imagine we have two slider-bars that change the world we know: one for the state of skyscraper technology, high-tech or lower, and the other for the political and economic climate. We'll start with a scenario that might seem counterintuitive: a sharp reaction against the trends of the past two decades.

In this scenario, today's variety of supertalls, those glossy spires of the wealthy gulf states and an emergent China with a lot to prove, are considered archaic failures. They are white elephants—stodgy, overwrought, beside the point. The baton of great construction has been passed to much younger cities, the world's biggest and fastest-growing urban clusters, in Brazil, India, and Africa. These cities struggle to house colossal floods of urban immigrants by the cheapest and fastest means possible.

They're not rich enough to burn money like oil, but they do have plenty of labor power, plus some new, digital means of social organization. The results are huge, pyramidal, and lopsided, rather than supertall, spindly, and elegant. These are crowd-funded super-favelas, a kind of Kowloon Walled City on steroids. These socially innovative yet low-tech structures are plug-in and pre-fab, fast-rising and poorly regulated, with an anarchic Internet philosophy of small pieces loosely joined. Ugly and cheap, yet immeasurably vast, they teem with human vitality. Power is solar and piezoelectric. Water and sewage are iffy. Streets are nameless. The police travel the crooked alleys in well-armed squadrons.

Peasant habits persist in little urban farms and chicken-coops. Scrappy, vernacular building methods are learned from video instructables, conveyed by open-source handheld devices. The building materials are recycled steel rebar and bleak microfiber cement, splashed with vivid tropical paints to break the monotony. Building Information Management is alien and unheard of. The locals pride themselves on the sort of ingenuity-under-duress known in India as *jugaad*—and on unashamed piracy. The bottom billions are a vast global majority, rising on crooked iron stairs.

In our second scenario, technology is similarly limited, but a different social logic prevails. It's sterner and more authoritarian in flavor, in established cities dominated by anxious people who feel they have a lot to lose. Violent weather is of grave concern. Seaside cities suffer storm floods, while tall towers suffer freak wind loads.

The newer style of tower is therefore fortress-like. These urban castles have a no-nonsense, mil-spec look: sturdy, dignified, and disciplined, with legible architectural features that visibly promise not to fall into pieces. These are not glossy showpieces for the public eye gazing up from the street. These panoptic towers are the high ground. They are watchtowers, and they surveil the city with care, using canny methods borrowed from the drone industry and social media surveillance marketing.

Management systems haunt every tower, and they're of an aggressive, suspicious design, fully integrated with city police and national intelligence services. The disgruntled have launched cyberwar attacks: by seizing digital control of the towers' tuned-mass dampers—anti-sway counterweight systems—enemies can swing the towers violently, terrifying the occupants with artificial earthquakes.

In our third scenario, Building Information Management is exceedingly advanced, and it has carried urban society with it toward a complex tech-nocracy. The watchwords here are software code, regulation, decency, fairness, justice, and endless niggling confrontations with the networked share-holders. Towers are colossal, but they're warped into weird shapes by demands for light rights and view-ing corridors. Luckily, parametric engineering is so advanced that buildings have little trouble contorting themselves to meet irrational political demands. Awkward and apologetic, these supertalls have museum-style, skeuomorphic detailing fit to please King Charles III.

Sustainable environmentalism has been baked into the regulations, aided and abetted by regulatory capture by the biggest global vendors. The rights delays can cause cost overruns, but the general financial picture for big building is sturdy and predictable. These towers rise slowly and steadily. They are great places to live on a pension: they're decent, healthy, well-lit, dependably serviced, and wheelchair-friendly, with eager tenant questionnaires twice a week.

In our last scenario, the Smart City has conquered all it sees. Architecture slavishly follows the postindustrial logic of the dominant titans of the era: Samsung, Apple, Huawei, Amazon, Google, Facebook. National and urban legal structures have been undercut, bankrupted, and disrupted by the great networks. The Dumb Cities of the past are proved archaic, just too slow—stumbling blocks routed around by the process flows. Humming cloud barns are the new factories, package distribution centers are the new megamalls. Fully privatized digital "enterprise zones" flourish in the once-hallowed city halls, while new supertalls have become prestigious follies for elaborate digital empires.

Bizarre experiments flourish. Everyday objects are unnecessarily digitized, in much the way that pencil sharpeners used to be streamlined. Walls and floors are made of ultralight carbon fiber, vibrating like drumheads. Elevators are fired up and down like big plastic bullets, and woe to the occupants' over-pressured ears. Touchscreen building skins act as monster billboards, where the rival skyscrapers flame and screech at one another. Little courier robots, zipping along on their generic Googlemaps, are becoming more common than rats.

Some towers go rent-free to occupants, if they're willing to abandon their privacy entirely to the prurient landlord. Augments haunt the halls and streets; it's considered chic to remove all the visible, touchable controls, restricting access to the handheld devices of tenants. Doorways, and even the sidewalks, argue with the derelicts, Siri-style.

This bounty of features comes at a price: severe instability and cruelly rapid obsolescence. Real estate is a casino; whole cities go bust with the slick invisible ease of Facebook annihilating MySpace. The City of Oz is splendid, but the Wizard of Oz, for all his greatness and power, is one phosphor-dot thick.

Building scenarios is rather like throwing tarot cards. The spirit of the times, the zeitgeist, is like one hand assembled from the deck of history. As with any card game, it's combinatorial, and multifactorial.

When a zeitgeist changes with the passing of years, it is not abolished or disproved forever; it merely retreats into the quiet darkness of the deck, awaiting future probabilities. A battle among four scenarios, like the ones I described here, is rather like a four-player poker hand. Yes, they're all mere gambles, mere speculations, yet they're not of equal value. Among those four, one will predominate.

A skyscraper is a multiplex, archetypal symbol, rather like some vast, freestanding Tarot card. A tower conveys a meaning, yet that meaning shifts with every new deal.

The Eiffel Tower is of particular interest here, not because it's new, but because it's so old. The Eiffel Tower has been a sideshow freak and also a treasured icon. It has been the steely product of the white-hot forge of high technology, and also a cherished antique. From its very birth, the Tower had admirers who wished it immortality, and even today, you could find a few Parisians who despise it, resent it, and wish it were gone. The steel and rivets Eiffel left may not change much, but we do. Then we surprise ourselves with our own perversity, gather the cards to our chests, and we pick up where we left off. All in the fullness of time.

Never Had People Lived in Such Aerial Splendor

Tom Vanderbilt

"Living in high-rises required a special type of behavior, one that was acquiescent, restrained, perhaps even slightly mad." So declares the protagonist (rather presciently, a producer of television documentaries) of J. G. Ballard's 1975 novel *High-Rise*, a dystopian fable, set in a tall luxury building outside central London, whose rational architecture and enveloping all-mod-cons embrace cannot ultimately contain the social rot within. Ballard, the self-declared cartographer of "inner space," diagnosed the maladies of this "small vertical city," whose residents "thrived on the rapid turnover of acquaintances, the lack of involvement with others, and the total self-sufficiency of lives which, needing nothing, were never disappointed." Here was a vast machine "designed to serve, not the collective body of tenants, but the individual resident in isolation." It was "civil inattention"–the sociologist Erving Goffman's phrase for the way people cohabiting dense environments studiously ignore each other–run amok.

Ballard, who lived in a small detached house in the anodyne suburb of Shepperton, had his own proclivities and prejudices, his suspicions of modern urban life. But *High-Rise*, like most of Ballard's "science fiction," hardly required huge leaps of imagination. The novel's protagonist, contemplating a documentary that would "look at the psychology of living in a community of two thousand people boxed up into the sky," goes on to declare: "All the evidence accumulated over several decades cast a critical light on the high-rise as a viable social structure, but cost-effectiveness in the area of public housing and high profitability in the private sector kept pushing these vertical townships into the sky against the real needs of their occupants."

This far from feverish speculation could have been ripped from a sociological journal of the day—or the headlines. Minoru Yamasaki's Pruitt-Igoe public housing complex in St. Louis was being slowly and spectacularly demolished. Residents in cities like San Francisco were resisting what they saw as a physical and psychic occupation of the city's soul by tall buildings (as one report noted, a survey of downtown office workers "showed a large percentage of them to feel personally *oppressed* by the buildings around them"). Critics such as Ada Louise Huxtable had charged that "perhaps the most appalling characteristic of the skyscraper is its inhumanity."[1] Films like *The Towering Inferno* depicted skyscrapers as the embodiment of reckless vanity by egomaniacal developers and narcissistic architects (images of the safari-jacketed Paul Newman, waving off nettlesome subordinates, repairing from his office to the adjoining boudoir, where Faye Dunaway beckons him toward the satin-sheeted bed).

Ballard himself was said to have been inspired by London's Trellick Towers, Erno Goldfinger's thirty-one-story tower block in North Kensington, completed in 1972 and almost instantly a symbol for urban social pathology (buildings like Trellick, or London's Alton Estate, notes critic Owen Hatherley, very quickly became the "mute, imposing backdrop" to the grim totalitarianism in François Truffaut's *Fahrenheit 451* and other films). As in *High-Rise*, in which the complex's architect himself occupies the structure's penthouse, Goldfinger actually briefly lived in the Trellick's predecessor building, the Balfron Tower, to "publicize its qualities."

1   Ada Louise Huxtable, "Towering Question: The Skyscraper." *The New York Times*, June 12, 1960.

The year Ballard's novel was published, I was seven years old and living in suburban Chicago. On trips to the city I would gaze with fascination, from the backseat of the family Monte Carlo, upon the two typologies of high-rise living. Situated at extremes of geography and demography, both were imposingly remote from and mysterious to my own split-level, single-family suburban mental maps.

First, arrayed along the Dan Ryan Expressway like a set of coastal bunkers, were the Robert Taylor homes, a bleak and unrelenting wall of twenty-eight hulking tower blocks, exterior hallways encaged like prison floors, their façades a flat expanse of dun-colored concrete, save for fire-scarred black shadows flaring from certain windows. In the city itself, just adjacent to the Loop on the banks of the Chicago River, were the two corn-cob-like silos of Bertrand Goldberg's Marina City, which looked to me like futuristic incubators for urban living. When completed in 1964, they were not only the world's tallest concrete structures, but also the tallest *residential* towers. Never—not even in the city where the sky-scraper was born—had people lived in such aerial splendor. Marina City's round shape was dictated by practical, floor-area-to-exterior-surface concerns; but also, according to Goldberg, something deeper. "[I] wanted to get people out of boxes, which are really psychological slums … those long hallways with scores of doors opening anonymously are inhuman. Each person should retain his relation to the core. It should be the relation of the branch to the tree, rather than that of the cell to the honeycomb."[2]

2   See Caroline Nye Stevens, "Marina City," in *Blueprint: Chicago*, January 21, 2011, accessible at http://www.blueprintchicago. org/2011/01/21/marina-city/.

Both the Robert Taylor Homes and Marina City were responses, in high concrete, to pressing mid-twentieth-century urban conditions: providing affordable housing, largely for the Great Migration of African Americans from the South to the North (with the spatial goal, as Nicholas Lehman notes in his book *The Promised Land*, "to keep as many of the migrants as possible apart from white Chicago"). Marina City was, arguably, the other side of the coin: an attempt to stem the departure of mostly white, higher-income residents from the central metropolis, a Corbusian Unité city-within-a-city with its own supermarket, a bowling alley, and, most excitedly to my juvenile mind, a circular parking garage twisting beneath the residents in the very same structure.

As it happened, the multi-story car park, too, was a source of dark fascination for Ballard. "One of the most mysterious buildings ever built," as his novel *Crash* (the predecessor to the 1996 film) declares. "Is it a model for some strange psychological state, some kind of vision within its bizarre geometry?" His next question could have been directed as much at high-rise living as high-rise parking: "What effect does using these buildings have on us?"

Why should we even think that high-rise living *has* an effect on us? One does not, after all, see detailed psycho-architectural studies of ranch houses. The primary reason may be sheer novelty. "Given the age of our species, living more than a few stories up is a very recent phenomenon," writes Robert Gifford in *Architectural Science Review*. "This tempts one to conclude that high rises are unnatural, and some would argue that what is unnatural must be, in some way, harmful."[3]

It is easy to find de facto condemnations of height, like this, from Christopher Alexander, in *A Pattern Language*: "In any urban area, no matter how dense, keep the majority of buildings four stories high or less. It is possible that certain buildings should exceed this limit, but they should never be buildings for human habitation." Alexander, verging into Ballard-esque territory, further warns: "The higher people live off the ground, the more likely they are to suffer mental illness."[4]

There seems to be a lingering, Babel-inflected mixture of awe and unease with the idea of "living in the sky." It is easy to look at the images in photographer Michael Wolf's book *The Transparent City* and see nothing but dehumanization, huge structures housing small Edward Hopper figures leading lives of collective solitude, nestled together in their separate window frames before our eyes like some split-screen narrative from an Altman film, but unknown to each other. In Ayn Rand's *Atlas Shrugged*, protagonist Dagny Taggart, sitting in her high, Roarkian office, looks at other distant skyscrapers, wondering from which one her would-be love interest might be watching her. "Just to know that you're seeing me, even if I'm never to see you again." Notions of public and private, distance and intimacy, are blurred in the age of the tall glass tower.

Perhaps there is something in height itself behind the blurring. As one of the authors in a collected 1977 volume, *Human Response to Tall Buildings*, noted: "How visual separation might

3   Robert Gifford, "The Consequences of Living in High-Rise Buildings," *Architectural Science Review*, 50, 1, p. 8.

4   Christopher Alexander, *A Pattern Language* (New York: Oxford University Press, 1977), p. 177.

relate symbolically to psychological separation cannot be guessed at this time." But he quotes the environmental psychologist Edward T. Hall: "At the distance people look like ants, contact with them as human beings fades rapidly." One thinks of the nefarious Harry Lime in *The Third Man*, in a Ferris wheel high above Vienna, looking down and asking Holly Martins, with cold contempt, "Would you really feel any pity if one those dots stopped moving forever?"

Conversely, people living in tall buildings tend to speak—perhaps not surprisingly, as they have chosen to live there—of the ennobling qualities of height. Early residents of the John Hancock building in Chicago (then, looking down on Marina City, the world's highest residents) described the sensation as "being in the country," or in the "fifth dimension." An advertising executive with children marveled how he was spending more time with his family now that his commute was simply down the elevator to the twenty-seventh floor. In one account, a resident, "having left a home in the suburbs for the tower, had taken an interest in nature *after* his move to the city. Now with his expansive view of lake and sky, he could watch the sun ride over the lake, the stars and moon in the sky, and the annual migration of birds."[5]

So how to square this with a body of research that seems to conclude that most people find high-rise living less satisfactory than low-level living; that tall buildings seem to breed more crime than their lower-situated counterparts; that small children seem to develop (by reading and other measures) less quickly the higher up they live; that tall buildings

---

5   Ezra Stoller, *The John Hancock Center* (New York: Princeton Architectural Press, 2000), p. 9.

might even invite suicide? Could an architectural form really *do* all that? Architecture is never more than a container for social relations. And so high-rise sociology is troubled by larger factors—who is living in the high-rise, and under what conditions? Pruitt-Igoe became synonymous with the problems of high-rise housing; it was considered the death knell of modernist social planning and modern architecture all at once. The backward, revisionist look has been more nuanced.

In Chad Friedrich's documentary film, *The Pruitt-Igoe Myth*, residents tenderly recall the "poor man's penthouses" they were moving into; of feeling safe surrounded by so many other sets of residents. But soon, the elevators stopped working, vandalism set in, strangers lurked in stairwells. Was there something inherent in its form that caused the decay to set in? Jane Jacobs argued that these tall buildings were "streets piled high in the sky," but without the public view ground-level streets enjoyed, and so lacking "the checks and inhibitions exerted by eye-policed city streets." Curiously, the equally lamented Trellick Towers—once as much a negative symbol as Pruitt-Igoe—have seen a remarkable turnaround: they are now a heritage-listed, increasingly desirable place to live. The turning point came in the early 1990s with the formation of a residents' association and the installation of front-desk security (a seeming no-brainer, per Jacobs, but something that was once frowned upon by the Greater London Council). Far from isolation, Trellick now seems to pulse with fellow-feeling. One resident makes a curious connection between community and height: "London sprawls below in all directions as far as the eye can see so maybe we need to know we're not alone up here."[6]

Much of the research about the problems of tall-building living is really research about, as the sociologist Gerda Wekerle put it, "the problems created by concentrating multiproblem families in housing stigmatized by the rest of society." Other studies have looked at the populations of places like dormitories, which are themselves hardly representative. The high-rise form is endlessly skewed by social extremes. As Wekerle argues, "Pruitt-Igoe is no more representative than is the John Hancock Center of high-rise living."[7] And then there's context. In places like Singapore or Hong Kong, tall-building living is not only the norm, it is considered socially prestigious. A friend who grew up on the nineteenth floor of an Upper East Side New York City apartment building (and who, interestingly, grew up to be an architecture critic) finds nothing odd, in retrospect, about his upbringing; most of his friends, after all, lived in similar circumstances, if not in the very same building. Why would you need a suburban lawn, he suggested, when Central Park was five minutes away? In terms of building height, he notes: "I don't think it really had much effect one way or another, perhaps because so many of the neighboring buildings were of relatively equal height, so there wasn't a sense of vertigiousness." For the record, he seems to read very well.

Of course, the nineteenth floor may begin to seem rather *low*-rise. All over the world, there has been a proliferation of very tall residential buildings. In New York City alone, these now range from Frank

6   Rory Carroll, "How did this become the height of fashion?" *The Guardian*, March 10, 1999.

7   From *Human Response to Tall Buildings,* edited by Donald J. Conway (New York: Downden Hutchinson & Ross, 1977), p. 230.

Gehry's seventy-six-story Spruce Street tower to Christian de Portzamparc's 1,000-foot-high One57 to Rafael Viñoly's nearly 1,400-foot tall 432 Park Avenue to SHoP's planned 1,400-foot-plus 111 West 57th Street, all of which will provide, when completed, the highest possible living-places in the Western Hemisphere. Granted, units in these "airplane view" structures may be more safe-haven pied-à-terre (which means, ironically, "foot to the ground") for the global one-percent than demographically main-stream housing. But everywhere there is a clear trend at work. In 2012, an estimated forty-one of the world's 100 tallest buildings were offices; a decade previously, the figure was twice that.

In the late 1970s, Fazlur Kahn, the structural engi-neer behind both the Sears (now Willis) Tower and the John Hancock Building, said: "Today, without any real trouble, we could build a 150-story building. Whether we will, and how the city will handle it, is not an engineering question, it is a social question."

A few decades later, Mark Lavery, an engineer with BuroHappold in Dubai, was asked, at a confer-ence on tall buildings, "What is the panel's view on the environmental psychology of tall buildings?" In his response, he evoked the spirit of Kahn, saying human response was really "the most fundamental topic facing the future of supertall buildings," that perhaps it is we who are "the only real barrier to how tall we will go."

The supertall building, as Lavery noted to me, comes with its own special set of engineering circumstances. Apart from the obvious differences in seismic and wind loads, there is the idea that more services need to be distributed further along a vertical core. Things we now take for granted—like

strong mobile phone connections–become strained
at height. Elevators, for the moment, are at their
limit: as they still rely on cables, the required hous-
ings simply become too large. And so we have
systems of "local" and "express" elevators, in which
users might have to change cars two or even three
times (satisfaction decreasing with each transfer)
just to reach or leave their homes. Elevator speeds
have increased to some fifty feet per second, though
Lavery suggests actual travel speeds may be lower.
People's discomfort seems to set in at above thirty
feet per second, and there is also, he suggests, a large
increase in cost for each minor increase in speed.
At a 2012 Council on Tall Buildings and Urban
Habitat conference, a property developer noted that
at the Shanghai Tower, the lifts travel fifty-nine feet
per second (by contrast, when Elisha Otis unveiled
his first elevator in 1857, this exciting new form of
vertical transport traveled forty feet per minute). But,
the developer noted, other things begin to happen at
speed: "You are losing about four percent of atmo-
spheric pressure for every 1,000 feet that you go up
in the building. Your ears are going to pop and there
is definitely going to be less air at the top of this lift
than where you started."

   Elevator comfort is merely one of the ways
engineering solutions are required to improve the
psychological experience of inhabiting tall buildings.
Wind effects grow more pronounced the higher the
building goes; while these are lessened by any
number of dampening technologies or architectural
changes to the building's profile, it is the human
factor that remains perhaps the most critical. Human
tolerance for "wind excited" buildings has been studied
in countless wind-tunnel experiments (one early
study surreptitiously vibrated an eye doctor's office

without informing visitors), with acceptable parameters laid out in the International Organization for Standardization's ISO 6897, "or Guide to the evaluation of the response of occupants of fixed structures, especially buildings and off-shore structure, to low frequency horizontal motion." Studies examining phenomena like "low frequency narrow-band random motion" have found that humans seem particularly susceptible to certain rhythms ("with 0.25 Hz and 0.50 Hz being the more provocative frequencies"). Individual thresholds vary–one person's sick-making motion might be another's gentle sway–and exposure is key: office workers, who would spend less time in a tall building, seem to tolerate more motion than residents. People walking experience less motion sensation than those standing (because, one study noted, "of the additional movement due to self-motion masking the sense of vibration"). Often, people seem to be looking out windows when they sense vibration (due to "involuntary body self-motion generating visual parallax while focusing on a far-field object against a near-field reference such as a window frame").

The presence of strong winds means that tall building residences, in general, do not have balconies or operable windows. Containment is one of the peculiar hallmarks of super-tall living. "I've known buildings where they haven't considered it and built buildings up to 500 meters [with balconies]," says Mark Lavery, "and they've had to go in and install alarm systems with automatic lock-in of doors to stop people from physically opening their doors on windy days." And while high floors are most prized–more view, less noise–there comes, suggests Lavery, a sort of limit where the view no longer begins to appreciably improve with greater height, and may in fact get worse. "There's the weather, and the view can get sort of warped, you start to lose your link to it. It doesn't look real anymore."

One wonders what psychological effects there might be to this earthbound living in the sky. As the architecture critic Joseph Giovannini observed, "Living on the sixtieth floor is different. There are no earthly sounds, no close-up details outside, not even trees—just the long view and then the drop." Astronauts on NASA's space shuttle Discovery, asked to draw three-dimensional cubes, drew them with shorter vertical dimensions when in the zero-gravity of space.[8] Might living in the sky also subtly influence one's perspective of space, distance, and height? Studies have shown that children, at twenty-five months of age, can transmit information gleaned from aerial views to make ground-level way-finding decisions; at twenty-one months, however, they cannot. Would children whose homes come equipped with aerial views have an edge?[9] It is known, for example, that people with a fear of heights—or even those without when shown images of people falling—will overestimate actual heights.[10]

Do acrophiles actually experience the opposite effect? Do lovers of great heights feel *closer* to the ground than they really are? Does one's apartment

8   Corinna Lathan, Zuyi Wang, Gilles Clement, "Changes in the vertical size of a three-dimensional object drawn in weightlessness." *Neuroscience Letters* 295, 1 -2 (December 2000), pp. 37 -40.

9   J. J. Reiser and E. A. Rider, "Young children's spatial orientation with respect to multiple targets when walking without vision." *Developmental Psychology* 27 (2001), pp. 97-107.

10 Elise M. Clerkin, et al., "Imagery and fear influence height perception." *Journal of Anxiety Disorders* 23, 2 (April 2009), pp. 381-86.

then feel larger the higher one goes up? And does this have to do with visual psychology or social psychology—the idea that you are living on top of so many others? Conversely, as Robert Gifford wonders, "Do people on lower floors experience the many floors above them as a sort of crushing burden?"

For now, we must still rely largely on anecdote. "I have a huge amount of space," said one resident of Gehry's 870-foot-high New York tower. "Not the square footage of my moderate one-bedroom, but the space all around me."[11]

11   Robin Finn, "The Stratospherians," *New York Times*, May 10, 2013.

An American Versailles

Matthew Yglesias

Washington, DC is the capital of the mightiest empire the world has ever known. It is a curious act that the seat of the government that invented the Internet, that sequenced the human genome, and that put a man on the moon is oddly averse to one particular aspect of modern technology: the skyscraper.

To be sure, the city is not innocent of the concepts of steel-frame construction or elevators. But it exists almost as if it were. Offices downtown are constructed with modern methods and modern conveniences. But they don't truly take advantage of them. Instead of the towers of a contemporary city, the central business district consists of slightly strange, squat structures—all wider than they are tall, and, generally, rectilinear rather than tapered. Twelve- or, more often, ten- or fewer stories high, they could have been built a hundred or more years ago.

The fans of the DC status quo flatter themselves to think that the low-slung profile lends the city a Parisian ambiance. This strikes me as an optimistic assessment of the aesthetics.

The fact, either way, is that DC is no Paris by a number of factors. Most importantly, central Paris is low-slung because it is well preserved. Downtown Washington, outside the immediate environs of the National Mall, is a thoroughly modern city. The short buildings around L'Enfant Plaza, Farragut Square, or Chinatown aren't classics of a bygone age. They're simply short. Even neighborhoods that essentially didn't exist until the twenty-first century— such as "NoMA" and Mt. Vernon Triangle—refuse to take advantage of the modern talent to stack several dozen floors atop each other without facing any crippling structural challenges.

This situation, so anomalous among major American cities, came to pass because of a backlash against the construction of the 164-foot Cairo Hotel (now an apartment building) way back in 1894.

The Cairo certainly was a tall building for its time, and is still a pretty large building for a quiet residential street in any city (it is well outside the CBD in Dupont Circle). That people at the time of its construction found it a bit alarming is natural, even forgivable. Cities all around the world had to respond then to the kind of concerns—crowding, access to daylight—such new buildings raised. The normal approach was to adopt codes limiting tall buildings to particular sections of the city, and generally to require some kind of tapering, or setback, to preserve light on the street below. In addition, high-rise construction required new kinds of rules about fire safety not formerly necessary.

But due to a strange quirk of history, in 1899, Congress chose to give the District not just a zoning code or a fire ordinance, but the Height of Buildings Act. This measure, modified slightly in 1910, caps downtown buildings at a height based on the width of the street they face. In general, this means the tallest buildings in the city are just 130 feet tall (a small section of Pennsylvania Avenue qualifies for heights up to 160 feet) with many downtown blocks limited to 110 feet or shorter.

It turns out that forcing a city to limit its buildings to nineteenth-century heights doesn't turn it into a nineteenth-century city. In particular, Washington's downtown office buildings generally come with underground parking garages and its inhabitants enjoy large modern dwelling spaces. Consequently, DC's 10,000 residents per square mile actually puts its population density closer to Fargo, North Dakota, than to a French capital that is over five times as dense. Last, but by no means least,

France has made a very deliberate effort to cope with the consequences of eschewing density by building an enormous skyscraper cluster just beyond the city limits in La Défense—no further from the Île de la Cité than the American University campus is from the Capitol.

Thus the true consequence of the stunting is less to make Washington into an American Paris than to force it to serve as an American Versailles, an exclusive community dedicated to ruling a country rather than being an integral piece of the country it rules.

Throughout the long years of urban divestment that followed the introduction of the automobile in the 1950s, the riots of the 1960s, and the crack epidemic and subsequent crime waves of the 1980s, the Height Act seemed perhaps not so significant. Relatively few people wanted to live in the District or build much of anything there. But the city, like so many other cities in America, turned itself around in the 1990s with a judicious mix of improved public policy, falling crime, and a renewed fashion for urban living.

Today the city is thriving. Indeed, with the imminent completion of the City Center project, located on the site of the former convention center (a new one has been built in a formerly residential area), the traditional downtown will be entirely built-out. Future real estate development schemes involve decking over I-395 or the railroad tracks leading into Union Station. But the thriving Washington coexists with a rather unhappy one—a blacker, more working class city disgruntled with festering high unemployment and terrified of gentrification and displacement. Thriving Washington has also become a source of substantial resentment at a time when the United States has been having a rough economic go of it.

Annie Lowrey's spring 2013 look at the region's boom for *The New York Times Magazine* was headlined "Washington's Economic Boom, Financed by You." Her colleague, the conservative columnist Ross Douthat, was even more pointed, labeling it "a city running on exploitation." David Leonhardt, the paper's Washington Bureau Chief at the time, said DC's prosperity "uncomfortably calls to mind the rapacious Capitol in Suzanne Collins's *Hunger Games* series."

It is true that average incomes in the DC metro area are among the highest in the country. But the cause here is less relentless expropriation than broad economic trends that have benefitted all American metropolitan areas with highly educated workforces. The regions surrounding Minneapolis, Boston, San Francisco, and Charlotte don't have an enormous amount in common, but they all share high median incomes and large numbers of college graduates.

Of course it's true that Washington is a mecca for educated people largely because the federal government is here. But this has very little to do with the expensive and politically controversial aspects of the government—Social Security, Medicare, Medicaid, Food Stamps, and the rest of the welfare state. These programs cost vast sums of money, but the money is paid out to citizens all across the country. Retirement hubs such as Florida and Arizona are, in this sense, much more dependent on the federal government than the DC area is.

No plausible small government agenda exists under which the Census Department will stop hiring statisticians, the Treasury Department will stop hiring economists, the FDA will stop hiring doctors, the Nuclear Regulatory Commission will stop hiring scientists, or the Department of Transportation will no longer need engineers. Nor will small government politics turn back the tide of history. The basic administration of government once required an army of middle class clerks. So many that Washington's Cardozo High School football field advertises itself as the Home of the Clerks. These days there is less need for filing and fetching and more need for a smaller, but higher-paid, set of information technology professionals, who are often private contractors. And since the basic work of government takes place in state capitals and county seats all across the country, DC-based firms actually serve a national marketplace as vendors of the tools of governance.

The truly regrettable thing about Washington in 2014 isn't that it's become prosperous. It's that it's become so exclusive.

In principle, a city full of relatively well-paid college graduates ought to also be a decent place to cook food or cut hair or drive a cab or fix cars or remodel kitchens or sell groceries or perform any of the myriad other service-sector jobs that account for the vast majority of employment in every American city. But if you rig the supply of inhabitable square footage, you naturally create a scarcity. Scarcity means high prices. And, indeed, Washington has become close to the top of the list for American cities in terms of housing prices, office rents, and hotel rooms. For the relatively small number of Americans with careers and skills specifically tied to the federal government, that's a price worth paying. But for everyone else, the prosperity of Washington is illusory, with any income gains immediately eaten away by higher prices.

Washington is hardly unique in having become underbuilt and overpriced. But the capital city of a country plays a unique role relative to other cities, and so it is particularly galling for it to be exclusionary. Even worse, the most prominent mechanism of exclusion—the Height Act—is a measure taken by Congress rather than the municipality.

If the national government is going to meddle in a city's affairs it should be to force a broader view of the national interest, not to play NIMBY from afar.

A Congress willing to repeal the act and open the city to tall, modern structures would do the country an enormous favor. The capital wouldn't cease to be prosperous. But unlike the Capitol of Collins' and Douthat's *Hunger Games* nightmares, it would be a beating heart of prosperity for the entire country rather than a refuge of a narrow elite.

Think of a London or Tokyo or Berlin—a thriving capital city that is a center of business and culture and not just government.

Americans are somewhat accustomed to the idea of dreary capital cities. We deliberately chose to establish our seat of government in a vacant swampland rather than in New York or Philadelphia, or even nearby Baltimore. And our state capitals are often in out-of-the-way spots—Albany or Sacramento—rather than thriving metropolises. But even at home we have the example of state capitals like Boston and Austin, multi-functional cities where politics is important to the local economy without dominating it.

Consider even simple tourism. Right now the market for downtown hotel rooms in Washington is expensive and overwhelmingly dominated by business travelers. Opening downtown to skyscrapers would lead to a surge of hotel rooms, and more affordable prices for families looking to visit the Smithsonian and the National Zoo. This would be a nice favor to an American population whose tax dollars support the attractions. It would also mean many more jobs in the hospitality industry, jobs available to working class people and those with skills outside the political sphere.

But the construction of skyscrapers downtown would have broader and more significant implications. In particular, as existing office buildings are replaced with much taller towers the fate of the remaining building stock will become interesting. The federal city really only needs so much office space, and, with proper buildings, that space could be provided with a quarter or less of the current footprint.

That would open up space for two key things the capital currently lacks. One is ample housing—apartments affordable to the middle class—and the other is office space that's not reserved for companies willing to pay a premium for access to the levers of political power.

The housing would, in effect, un-gate the city, opening its doors to all Americans. *The Hunger Games* is not a tract on economic geography. But it's clear that the only way to maintain the systematic inequality between the residents of the rich capital and the poor coal mining culture of District 12 is to prevent people from moving. And, of course, this is precisely what authoritarian governments around the world do. Controls on internal population movements were integral to the Soviet social and economic system, and despite reforms a similar system known as *hukou* still rules the day in China. In pre-modern Europe, peasants were often tied to specific tracts of land and tsarist Russia restricted Jews to living within a delineated Pale of Settlement.

The United States, conversely, has always been a land of opportunity in part because people have been able to move to opportunity.

That's the story of immigration to the New World, of course. But it's also the story of the Great Migration of African-Americans away from the sharecropping economy of the Jim Crow South and toward the wider vistas of northern cities. It's the California Gold Rush of 1848 and the settling of the western frontier as people struck out from the homes in search of affordable farmland. People living in communities that have been negatively impacted by economic trends would, of course, prefer for those problems to simply go away. But picking up and moving has always been a good second option. And yet, the rate of internal geographic migration in the United States has fallen nearly in half since the beginning of the 1990s. The reasons for this are partly demographic—the country is older now—but the waning availability of affordable housing in high-income areas is another large factor.

Bringing high-rise apartments to the center of the capital city would only make a partial dent in a national problem. But it would be a powerful statement of principle, as well as a constructive step in its own right.

Last, but by no means least, allowing office towers downtown would bring DC more office space. One of the main reasons why the city attracts a demographic some imagine to be "parasitic" is that unlike many national capitals, America's capital houses very few nationally recognized firms that aren't related to the business of governing. This, however, isn't for a lack of talents or ideas. Instead, it's a consequence of the high cost of doing business. If your company lobbies Congress or litigates before regulatory agencies, then high rents are a small price to pay for direct access to the federal institutions. But companies with other kinds of ideas tend to end up fleeing. The handful of exceptions, such as the daily deals website Living Social, tend to persist only thanks to generous tax subsidies offered by the city government—subsidies that can only scale so far. A Washington dotted with skyscrapers would have much less scarcity of square footage, and much more opportunity for firms to grow and thrive no matter what line of work they're in.

Put it all together, and a taller Washington, DC would be a much healthier city. Today, it's a mid-sized, high-income, exclusionary metropolis with an economic monoculture. But it could become a diverse giant that serves as an engine of economic opportunity for people all throughout the country. But to get there, it needs to dream big—just as its founders did—and get ready to build bigger.

The Form Could Be Reborn
Diana Lind

If not the most powerful corporation in America today, Facebook is arguably the most representative. The motto of its CEO, Mark Zuckerberg, is to "move fast and break things"—a call for the kind of disruption that defines our age. We all know how Facebook has disrupted what now seem like quaint forms of friendship, communication, information, and even voyeurism. But more than that, Facebook, along with all the start-up successes of Silicon Valley, has also disrupted paradigms of success and power. No longer is the American Dream defined by the idea of becoming a millionaire; now we dream of becoming billionaires before thirty. The reward of hard work is not to retire early, but to work long hours on a corporate campus that feels like Club Med. Not surprisingly, these disruptions have caused a shift in the aesthetics that signal power and success: where once it was suits and skyscrapers, now it's hoodies and coffee shops.

When Facebook sought to build a headquarters, it didn't build big and tall as General Motors once did in Detroit, as Citigroup did in New York, or even as CCTV did in Beijing. Instead, it reused an old Sun Microsystems suburban park, and with the help of consultants from Disney, turned it into a corporate campus with the ambience of a New Urbanist town. The campus is centered around a faux Main Street and spread across low-slung buildings. Conference spaces feature garage doors that hark back to companies and bands spawned in suburban garages. Cafes and bench-lined corridors provide ample opportunity for the kind of serendipitous encounters that business gurus all claim will generate great ideas. The campus has many of the amenities of a small town, such as a bike shop, a dry cleaner, a candy store—though these are all owned and operated by Facebook.

This casual atmosphere suggests the corporation is anything but corporate—like a selfie that's been Photoshopped to look insouciantly impromptu, but was actually very carefully staged. The Main Street aesthetic slyly encourages Facebook's workers to think that their office isn't an isolated compound but a community, that that round-the-clock work doesn't impinge upon an employee's personal life, that a corporate campus and a small town are nearly the same thing. This kind of deceptive architecture, devoid of theory but heavy on fantasy, has become not just the norm but a vogue of our times.

Multiplying the ground plane as they do, skyscrapers are by definition highly efficient spaces. Their design often seems to boast about their productivity and importance. Tall buildings as we know them were born of a time when Modernism swept not just architecture but all kinds of art. Modernists sought to develop a deep connection between form and function, the removal of deceptive ornament, a rationale or theory behind all aesthetic choices. This period, in which the skyscraper thrived and was perhaps its greatest emblem, aspired, in other words, to authenticity—a visual authenticity reflecting the frank expression of economic and cultural power.

While contemporary aesthetics may profess to aspire to authenticity, the real and the sincere are often confused today with a fetishization of the past. Twenty-somethings who grew up in the suburbs now inhabit cities, grouping in places like Williamsburg and Wicker Park, and they bring with them a new aesthetic, a kind of urban pastoral. Urbanites who may once have scoffed at McMansions built to mimic the great nineteenth-century homes of Edwin Luytens, now wear handlebar mustaches and suspenders—or they go punk, pretending to live in the

1880s or the 1980s. Like Facebook's campus, they search for the authentic by imitating it, not, as the modernists wished to, achieving it in a new, fitting, contemporary way.

As the urban pastoral aesthetic takes hold, contemporary design languishes; it has been consigned to trendy houses, IKEA furniture, and, of course, the skyscraper. Facebook's campus—and the nostalgic interiors of restaurants, cafes, clothing stores, and offices in New York, San Francisco, and other cities—suggest that the best money can buy today is the simulacrum of a bygone time.

This looking backwards would not be a problem if the values of the aesthetic fantasy were helping in some way to move our society forward. But it's not. At a time of increasing resource scarcity and environmental stress, we should be shunning office parks like that of Facebook's, built a ninety-minute car commute from the urban core where most of its employees live. With population growth and rising rents showing no sign of abating, low-density, New Urbanist designs simply cannot accommodate the demand of more than seven billion people on the planet.

Skyscrapers continue to be built—out of practical necessity, most often, or sometimes personal or governmental whim—but they are no longer in sync with the aesthetic desires of our new class of business leaders. Until this state of affairs changes, we will be hamstrung in our efforts to change our cities to meet the demands of changing times. How, then, can this density-generating typology, which has the potential to contribute so much to solving many of our economic, social, and environmental issues simultaneously, recapture the imaginations of our new young business leaders? How can the skyscraper return as an icon of our times?

Driverless cars, wearable computing, and the end
of personal privacy define the near-future reality in
which we live. If anticipatory buzz is any indication,
it appears we quite welcome a world where cars
drive themselves and every movement is tracked
with geospatial and personal data. And yet, despite
how much some of us love our apps and iPads, the
same people who lose themselves in their screens are
the ones who most need a connection back to the
human scale.

While you would think that our tech-utopian
future would provoke a strong and specific aesthetic
response—akin to people dressing in all black like
The Matrix, living in uncluttered homes like that
of *The Jetsons*, or even a more marked resurgence
of the mid-century Modern styles that evoke the
optimism of the Space Age—the facts suggest otherwise. The enduring architectural symbols of our times
aren't the icons by Rem Koolhaas or Frank Gehry,
with their often futuristic constructions and material,
but rather landscape architecture like The High
Line, the influential quasi-public park in Manhattan,
built on the preserved bed of an abandoned rail
line. This keening for the natural, however artificial
it may be in practice, should not surprise us: as our
cultures become more urban, our cities more dense,
the urge for a suburban and pastoral existence grows
ever more profound. As much as we want—and
even now need—to live a hybrid virtual/real existence,
we remain hungry for the warmth and humanity
of the past.

That is something we might find comfort in,
the retreat to the known values of a past, whether
Main Street or Mason jars, deemed to be authentically
physical. But when this hunger for substance is
expressed as a resistance to innovative architecture

that can sensibly and responsibly increase the density of our cities, it is having a deleterious effect on our shared future.

We've already seen in practice the consequences of the contemporary resistance to the new. As one of his last acts in office, former New York City mayor Michael Bloomberg fought to upzone (increase the potential density of) the area of Manhattan known as Midtown East, allowing that already well-sky-scrapered area to host even taller skyscrapers. His unsentimental approach–insensitive to wider anti-urban cultural forces–was met with great opposition (some of it for good reasons, as the plan was not fully thought through in terms of its effect on transit capacities and pedestrian-level quality of life). Yet New York grows ever more expensive because its supply of new space cannot keep up with the voracious demand by those who want to live and work there. Economists like Ed Glaeser point out that no small amount of affordable housing or inclusionary zoning will stem escalating housing prices; massive amounts of new housing, which would have to be built in tall buildings or residential skyscrapers, would be the only solution.

Still, compared to other cities, New York is relatively welcoming of increased density; in San Francisco, Boston and similar cities–where the identity of the cities themselves is contingent on quaint neighborhoods, and quaint neighborhoods command the highest prices–the resistance to accommodating growth through increased height is much greater. People's hatred of skyscrapers is on ample display in the fights that erupt whenever a tall building is proposed in a historically low-rise community. The NIMBYs inevitably claim that the new buildings will create long shadows, devalue adjacent properties, include insufficient parking, or simply bungle the look of the place. On an emotional level, many people still equate high-rise buildings with ill-fated housing projects, bad midcentury monumentality, and, on a subliminal level, the racial tensions that decimated inner cities at the time such buildings were being built. And perhaps not surprisingly, a person's opinion of density often depends on their age, race, and economic standing. A poll conducted recently in Santa Monica, California—a low-rise city where development is hotly contested—showed that older whites were in favor of height restrictions limiting new construction, whereas younger Latinos overwhelmingly welcomed less restricted growth.

From Jane Jacobs to Andres Duany, the father of New Urbanism, there have been persuasive arguments against skyscrapers, arguments for encouraging smaller-grained urban environments that promote varied uses and respect the human scale. Such theorists have long argued, and I would have to agree, that the traditional proportions of a well-tempered street resonate intrinsically with the human body and mind. We can sometimes see this environmental preference expressed as an economic fact-on-the-ground. To continue using New York City as an example, the area of Manhattan east of Park Avenue and north of 23rd Street remains markedly less expensive than other comparable neighborhoods in the city, such as the Upper West Side. While the East Side offers good transit, plentiful public space, relative safety, and access to schools and the other amenities that tend to drive up real estate prices, it also is home to the highest concentration of Manhattan's least-beloved mode of high-rise architecture. In the era where the urban pastoral aesthetic reigns, a forty-story white brick building from the 1960s lacks curb appeal.

Those who can choose, the workforce of the New Economy foremost among them, have chosen to live elsewhere. Brooklyn's brownstone neighborhoods command ever-higher prices. It would seem that the lower-scaled, tree-lined, coffee shop-dotted streets that have come to define the Brooklyn renaissance are the ideal setting for a generation of newly declared urbanites, reacting to the suburbs of their youth while seeking out the authentic experience of the real as a necessary counterpoint to their full-on immersion in the digital.

But there are factors beyond taste that have caused tall buildings to be reflexively maligned. Skyscrapers, with their typically more spacious dimensions—and with the pressures on developers to make their construction pay—are more likely to house a sterile chain drug store or bank on the ground floor than a cool new bar. The same economic pressures, the simple requirements of thrift associated with profitable development, mean that more often than not, new, tall construction is not a showcase for innovative design. Instead, we see bland coloration, a lack of striking detail, poor lighting, the same old rectangular shape, and pitiful public spaces—in New York often a trade-off for increased height—that almost seem to mock the public realm. While they may offer great amenities to their residents, such skyscrapers can be deadly on the street.

And thus, in every city, a cycle begins: neighborhoods with a large number of newer skyscrapers become soulless and bland, and so fewer people are attracted to these kinds of buildings. So skyscrapers become disassociated from the mainstream zeitgeist, from both a city's and our society's culture as a whole, from the very group–the growing, tastemaking cohort of authenticity-seeking young urbanites–that it is perhaps most important to habituate to high-rise living if our cities are to be reshaped to meet the challenges ahead. Certainly the residential and commercial towers of the type going up in certain New York City neighborhoods can fulfill the needs of many; young families, old people, young graduates, and value-driven renters and owners have long found these neighborhoods entirely suitable. But, by and large, for the group that matters most, the would-be denizens of the urban pastoral, tall buildings are an unappealing means to an end.

Despite being out-of-step with contemporary trends in urban living, despite our resistance to actually living in them, for nearly everyone, skyscrapers still foster a sense of delight. While we may at times evince a cultural dislike, even a hatred for them, tall buildings remain the preeminent symbolic touchstones of our cities. Drive toward nearly any city and once the skyline of downtown comes to the horizon, you know you have arrived. Even the city-loving but high-rise-eschewing resident of Wicker Park knows she is home when the Willis (formerly Sears) Tower rears above the prairie horizon, just as a Googler may welcome the sight of the Transamerica Pyramid across the bay. Many downtowns where the skyscrapers exist are inhospitable by day and desolate by night (e.g., Dallas, St. Louis, Cleveland, etc.), yet from afar at least, they remain at the heart of each city's self-image. A quick sketch of New York's skyline still defines the city, summing up its vitality much faster, and more thrillingly, than the image of a brownstone stoop.

How to close this gap, then, between the ongoing romantic appreciation of skyscrapers and their practical unpopularity? How to resolve a resistance to implementing them that may come to compromise our ability to build density-promoting tall buildings in the numbers that are necessary to house a growing, increasingly urbanized world?

Perhaps style is a place to start. A century ago, as architects became fed up with the gaudy—declaring styles such as the Art Deco and Art Nouveau to be representations of economic and even moral falsity—they pursued instead an architecture of more honest materials and forms. This was the glassy, spare style promoted by the Bauhaus School and eventually popularized as the International Style, the style of the first generation of modern skyscrapers. The most famous names of the era imbued their work with theory. Mies van der Rohe, architect of the Seagram Building and celebrated residential towers on Chicago's Lake Shore Drive, sought to have his architecture convey clarity, simplicity, and honesty, to break free of reliance on the conventions of ornament. Le Corbusier famously called houses "machines for living." Modern architecture, whether in the form of a skyscraper or a home, was meant to convey the image of productivity and round-the-clock activity that came to represent the pulsating metropolis of the first half of the twentieth century.

Eventually the efficiency of those skyscrapers came to represent the crudeness of capitalism. As skyscrapers became more plentiful and banal, their stock declined. But a century after skyscrapers first became part of the visual identity of cities, there is a prime opportunity for us to capitalize on their indisputable place in communicating the meaning of a city for a new era, their potential to redefine the aesthetics of our age. What is our other choice? To copy the limited virtues of the Facebook campus? To pastoralize our urbanized places? To deny the use of tall buildings in urban planning even as we need them more than ever to meet urban needs?

It is imperative that a new theory for skyscrapers be developed, one that will accommodate our culture's values. First and foremost, the Modernist notion of connecting form and function must be decoupled. After the attacks of September 11th, 2001, several design competitions were held to reimagine the World Trade Center site. One proposal called for a framework evoking the Twin Towers to be rebuilt out of an open, lattice-like steel structure. Rather than fill the buildings with office space, this plan, by a team of designers called THINK, proposed that cultural institutions and memorial spaces would occupy a few floors of the buildings' otherwise empty silhouettes. The surpassing popularity of this proposal— a rare moment of public consensus in that fraught redevelopment process—suggested that people loved, and even needed, the iconic stature of the sky-scraper. Its function, not so much. The THINK plan was declared the winner of its competition, a decision only overturned by direct intervention of political forces defending an economic status quo.

Is there a way to capture that sense of wonder we all feel when looking at a city skyline? To transfer it to the street level, to the public plaza underneath these towers, to the expression of the exterior of the building? Is there a way to leverage that enduring and affecting romantic attachment to tall buildings in order to make possible doing what is right for our cities?

The roof garden at the Lever House. The detailing at the top of the Chrysler Building. Even the Marina Bay Sands buildings in Singapore, with its infinity-edged pool spanning the roofs. These interventions suggest ways of reinventing a skyscraper so that it can be as enjoyable as a park—ways to build tall that may be seen to be as exciting as the newest side-street restaurant in some cozy urban pastoral neighborhood. The very size of a skyscraper may be a virtue here, offering limitless opportunities to adapt its form and appearance to new conditions—but only if architects reconsider the type, question the monoculture of its use, design it entirely anew, from the spire all the way down to the sidewalk. It may not be *that* we build tall, but *how* we do it, that has removed the skyscraper so far from the central place in our culture it once enjoyed.

One admirable aspect of the urban pastoral aesthetic, one that deserves to be retained, is the trend toward incorporating nature into urban life. Vertical farming is now a hot trend, but even a less ambitious wall garden can be deployed to mediate a tall building's necessary presence. In cities from Bangkok to Rio to Paris, there are examples of lush wall gardens that soften the buildings at street level and captivate pedestrians who might otherwise bridle at the intrusion. Rethinking the materials traditionally used in tall buildings—away from glass and steel, toward timber (another burgeoning trend) and new ecologically-friendly synthetics—is another possible means by which we can bridge the gap between the tastes and values of those who favor the urban pastoral, and the pressing imperatives of the urban present and future.

It would also be intriguing if we could find a way to not just amplify the playfulness of the skyscraper—as we've seen in recent years all over the world—but to reinforce its functional relationship to twenty-first-century forms of business. Today, most skyscrapers tend to house the headquarters of an enterprise, its intellectual capital, while the production line and the call-center are in far-flung, often suburban locales. But what if the skyscraper came to embody the sites of manufacturing? If the economics can be cracked, perhaps skyscrapers could also be used as bases for the aggregation of thousands of freelancers—already thirty percent of the American workforce is self-employed and that figure is just going to grow—instead of monocultural homes for a single, large company. If the skyscraper can evolve to catch up with modern work trends, it will be exciting to see how it will have to morph its form—to function as a factory, an enormous cafe for people working from laptops, something else we haven't yet dared to dream.

Skyscrapers, reimagined, could serve again as icons. Adapted minutely to contemporary conditions—the bio-engineering that will be necessary to live at modern standards during this period of climate change, the resource scarcity and population increase we must accommodate, the technological overlay of nearly every aspect of existence—the form could be reborn. But first they must recapture some of their lost allure as a significant cultural object.

The best way to do that may be to rediscover and exploit the skyscraper's virtues of honesty and pragmatism, to offer an alternative narrative of the future at a time when we're all falling for the fantasy of the past. If the ecological basis of increasing densification were more widely understood, living and working in a skyscraper could become a statement of environmentally savvy pride every bit as appealing as those the urban pastoral generation currently embraces. They could become symbols of the rejection of denial—the kind of denial that is palpable in office parks, served only by cars, which are secluded from the rest of the world.

As I write, Facebook has begun releasing official images of an expansion to its Menlo Park campus. Plans center around a new building by Frank Gehry. Occupying nearly twenty-two acres, reaching seventy-five feet high, and practically sunken under an enormous roof deck, it is a single room for thousands of Facebook's engineers, a sprawling new space in an urban sprawl we can no longer afford to promote. In the past, Gehry's buildings have been inspired by sailboats, ice hockey, the Italian baroque. This one reminds me of a skyscraper laid to rest, though not yet fully interred. It could still be resurrected.

Isenshard

Will Self

Shortly after the topping-out ceremony for Renzo
Piano's skyscraper, the Shard–which, at the time of
writing, is, at 1010 feet, the tallest building in
Europe–a squib appeared in the British satirical
magazine *Private Eye*. There's a regular feature in the
Eye called Lookalikes that invites readers to send
in two photographs which foreground a resemblance
between disparate people. Usually one of the individuals will be a politician or similar worthy and the
other a popular entertainer, so the intent is obvious:
to denigrate the former by association with the latter.
The images are always accompanied by the reader's
letter which follows a stock formula: "has anyone
else noticed the resemblance between X and Y, I
wonder if by any chance they may be related?" So it
was that a postage-stamp sized photo of the Shard
appeared, next to an equally grainy illustration of
the four-pronged tower inhabited by the wizard
Saruman in J. R. R. Tolkien's fantasy novel, *The Lord
of the Rings*; and the reader's letter of course read:
"has anyone else noticed the resemblance between
the Shard and Isengard, I wonder if by any chance
they may be related?"

Setting to one side fantastical nit-picking–
Isengard is the name of the entire fortress, the
central tower is, in fact, called Orthanc–this struck
me as a very funny trope indeed, and I'm still laugh-
ing. Like all the best visual jokes this one establishes
an antinomy; perceptually the two objects are
indeed startlingly similar, but conceptually they
couldn't be further removed. Or could they? What
makes the joke continue to resonate is the way
the mind goes on bouncing between the two towers,
delineating a complex interlacing of correspon-
dences, until forced to the conclusion that, yes, they
must indeed be related.

When it comes to skyscrapers I am, in the proper
sense of the word, ambivalent: I hate them for all
the obvious reasons—sometimes a cigar may be just a
cigar, but a skyscraper is always a big swaying phallus
vaunting the ambitions of late capitalism to reduce
the human individual to the status and the proportions of a submissive worker ant. Architecturally,
skyscrapers are the most meretricious of structures;
predicated not on the possible realization of any
aesthetic ideal, but on the actualization of specific
construction technologies. In syllogistic lockstep with
Mount Everest—which was climbed simply "because
it was there"—they are there … simply because.
And following on from the cast iron frame method
that allowed for the first skyscrapers to be raised
in the late nineteenth century, each successive wave
of innovation has been incorporated into further
erectile capability. The current architectural zeitgeist,
whereby form invariably follows finance, finds its
purest expression in the skyscrapers *de nos jours*,
which, with their parametrically designed waveforms,
positively billow with opportunism.

Yet I also love them—truly. I love their Promethean
swagger and their crystallization of the urbane.
I love their ability to transform our perception of the
city by proposing a new parallax around which we
instantly reorient as we tunnel along at ground level.
And I love the way that they are seemingly pur-
pose-built to accompany what Marshall McLuhan
limned as the "instantaneous medium" of electricity.
By day the Shard is an almost frantically undis-
tinguished building; far from being the mirrored
sliver thrust into the skyline its designer envisaged,
its dirt-dappled haunches hunker down on top
of London Bridge Station, surely straining even the
notable credulity of the City commuters who,

morning and evening, gaze up at the prosaism of
its exposed giant bolts. But by night, through the window of the bedroom where I sleep–a room I have
moved to simply to enjoy it–I thrill to the sight of this
Orion's dagger, dropped from the jet-howling darkness to quiver and wink in the sodium-lit belly of
the urban beast; and I hearken–like the good global
tribalist that I am–to the message of this medium,
which is that to look upon the Shard is, perforce, to
worship it.

I am a child of two cities with markedly different
edifice complexes. My mother was a New Yorker
who grew up in Queens; my father, a Londoner,
born in the southern suburb of Blackheath. As they
were growing up in the 1920s and '30s, both would
have had good long-distance views of their respec-
tively burgeoning metropolitan centers, with this
key difference: until the late 1960s, Wren's St Paul's
remained far and away the most salient building on
the London skyline, a baroque salver cover beneath
which lay church and state disjointed. London had
an early flirtation with the skyscraper: Queen Anne's
Mansions in Petty France, Westminster, was raised at
first to twelve stories in 1873 and a further two were
added in the early 1890s. Equipped with hydraulic lifts by its enterprising developer, Henry Alers
Hankey, the Mansions were at once a cynosure of
the new urban lifestyle–tenants included Sir Edward
Elgar–and a focus of the most intense disapproval,
not least from Queen Victoria, whose Royal prerog-
ative, she felt, included an unobstructed view of the
Houses of Parliament from her own back garden.
The architectural historian Harold Clunn said
of the Mansions, "it is for real ugliness unsurpassed
by any other great building in all London." The
1894 London Building Act, with its eighty-foot height

limit, was a direct result of this genteel disapproba-
tion; an ordinance that remained in place until it
was waived in 1963–essentially by Harold Wilson's
prime-ministerial fiat–so as to allow Conrad Hilton
to raise his Park Lane hotel to twenty-eight stories
(313 feet). When I was a child, in the 1960s and '70s,
central London remained a mostly low-rise zone,
with Millbank Tower, the Shell Centre, and Harry
Hyams's Centre Point (designed by Richard Sieffert)
being the notable exceptions.

Whereas in the United States the popular
perception of the skyscraper coalesced in a nimbus
around the International Style office block, in Britain
the field remained clear for the late-arrival of Le
Corbusier's machines for living: system-built structures (many prefabricated by the French engineering
company Camus), that came stalking ashore in the
late 1950s and early '60s. Initially hailed in the spirit
their planners intended–as harbingers of the new,
the classless and the progressive–the collapse of
Ronan Point, a twenty-two-story residential tower in
Newham, East London, in 1968, marked a definitive
break between optimistic postwar futurism and the
subsequent enduring association in British popular culture between the high-rise and high levels
of social anomie–a linkage that had already been
welded by Anthony Burgess's 1962 dystopic novel *A
Clockwork Orange*, with its urine-smelling and graf-
fiti-bedizened high-rises. This seems woefully unfair:
Ronan Point collapsed almost certainly because of
construction errors, but underlying any consideration of the practical merits of these buildings lay the
deep-rooted conflict between Ebenezer Howard's
bucolical, and low-rise, Garden City movement and
its Modernist rivals–a conflict that goes back to
at least the period when Queen Anne's Mansions

humped up above the horizon; when, in cultural form, it was played out in the oppositional views of the city enshrined on the one hand in the scientific romances of H. G. Wells, and on the other by the retro-feudal fantasizing of William Morris's *News from Nowhere.*

No Wellsian prospect of the distant future is complete without a full complement of mega-structures; he understood with deep and intuitive force that the technological extension of human capabilities would brook no opposition: an urbanism defined by the high-piling of the species was a prop-ositional inevitability of the form "Have pile driver, will drive piles." Wells's recasting of vertical living arrangements as expressive of vertiginous social hierarchies—which is seen most famously in his time traveler's confrontation with the surface-dwelling Eloi and their troglodytic nemesis, the Morlocks—becomes a familiar trope in the European popular culture of the early twentieth century. Fritz Lang's beautifully realized *Metropolis* is as much a celebra-tion of the penthouse and the roof garden as it is a bitter conflation of Taylorization with child-sacrificing despotism. The British disaffection from the high-rise as an instrument of social change—up-thrusting the proletariat—becomes, post-Ronan Point, subject to a spatial *bouleversement* by the razing of these skyscrapers. To take Merseyside as just one example, some eighty blocks were demol-ished in a twenty year period from the mid-1980s to the mid-2000s. For a while, in 2003–04, I had the tenancy of the highest flat in Liverpool; from the twenty-third story of this block in back of Lime Street Station I could see as far as Mount Snowden, seventy miles to the south. All around me extended the echoic emptiness not only of the block itself—that

by then had fewer than a hundred residents—but
the city as well, which had lost over half its population since 1945.

I had been allocated the apartment as part of
an art project, and typing a novella on my manual
machine in its gutted shell, I was conscious of acting
out an adaptation of J. G. Ballard's *High Rise* (1975).
Ballard's novel recasts the spatial analogue of class
warfare ingrained in the British popular imagination
of the skyscraper as a picaresque for the age of evolutionary psychology. The opening line is a synecdoche:
"Later, as he sat on his balcony eating the dog, Dr.
Robert Laing reflected on the unusual events that
had taken place within this huge apartment building
during the previous three months." The eponymous
high rise, in a familiar instance of Ballard's prescience, has been built on the Isle of Dogs site soon
to be occupied by One Canada Square (popularly
known as Canary Wharf), the blank-faced fifty-story
block designed by Cesar Pelli that became in the
1990s the concretization of London's financial Big
Bang, synonymous with the full alignment of British
society with Neoliberal finance capitalism—and
the concomitant eastward expansion of the City of
London—and which remained the tallest building in
Britain until the completion of the Shard. Ballard's
building is socially stratified, with the less affluent
tenants on the lower floors, and the penthouse
occupied by the architect-developer himself. As class
warfare breaks out between lower and upper floors,
and the building becomes willfully sealed-off from the
surrounding city, the protagonist, Laing, embarks on
a journey upwards that is less an exercise in social
climbing than a phylogenetic descent from the crown
of the evolutionary tree to its roots in primitivism.
Hence the dog roast.

Ballard's understanding of the role played by the skyscraper in the collective unconscious is that it cannot help–because of its alteration of the traditional proportions of domestic life–subsisting in an explicatory mode. In this he follows Levi-Strauss who observed that "all distortions in scale sacrifice the sensible in favor of the intelligible." Whether very small (an architect's model of a skyscraper) or very large (the skyscraper itself), the important factor is the loss of the felt experience. Of course, the actual myths that enshroud the cloudy summits of multi-story buildings are necessarily banal in secular Britain, quite as much as they are in the more plangent and religiously revanchist climate of the US. Nevertheless, Huxley when he opens *Brave New World* by limning the Central London Hatchery as "A squat grey building of only thirty-four stories"; Orwell, when he embeds the Ministry of Truth in a repurposed version of London University's Senate House (the tallest unconsecrated building in prewar Central London); Wells, Morris, Burgess; Ballard himself: all are operating within the unified field of the same foundational myth–

And the whole earth was of one language, and of one speech. And it came to pass, as they journeyed from the east, that they found a plain in the land of Shinar; and they dwelt there. And they said one to another, Go to, let us make brick, and burn them thoroughly. And they had brick for stone, and slime had they for mortar. And they said, Go to, let us build us a city and a tower, whose top *may reach* unto heaven; and let us make us a name, lest we be scattered abroad upon the face of the whole earth. And the Lord came down to see the city and the

tower, which the children of men builded. And
the Lord said, Behold, the people *is* one, and
they have all one language; and this they begin
to do: and now nothing will be restrained from
them, which they have imagined to do. Go to, let
us go down, and there confound their language,
that they may not understand one another's
speech. So the Lord scattered them abroad from
thence upon the face of all the earth: and they
left off to build the city. Therefore is the name
of it called Babel; because the Lord did there
confound the language of all the earth: and from
thence did the Lord scatter them abroad upon
the face of all the earth.

–a myth that remained indissolubly bound-up with
all Westerners' apprehension of the multi-story until
the morning of September 11th, 2001. Any and all
skyscrapers were at one and the same time worthy
anthropic subversions of the Godly perspective–
attempts to realize the entirety of human life within
the built environment–and hubristic affronts to our
Maker and his transcendent Will, for: "now nothing
will be restrained from them, which they have imagined to do." The British dichotomies bucolic/urban,
high-rise/low-rise, proletarian/bourgeois–all are mere
spin-offs, subsumed to this primary one–our will/His–
and its moral concomitant: good/evil. Naturally it follows, *mutatis mutandis*, God's razing of the Tower of
Babel recapitulates that earlier toppling from a peak
perspective, Lucifer's jump, and its sequel: the apple
of knowledge plummeting from a higher branch of the
phylogenetic tree down into Eve and Adam's moist-
ened mouths as they loiter between its roots.

The starts and fits with which skyscrapers were
raised in the US. may have been a response to

boom-and-bust economic cycles, while the Metternich-inspired floor plans of the late nineteenth-century skyscrapers—featuring individual worker-bee cells, each equipped with its own electric lighting, window and ventilation—served a sanitary conception of social advance; the buildings' hydraulic elevators literally lifted their clerkly tenants out of disease. However, New York's 1916 Zoning Resolution (unlike London's late Victorian stricture) imposed only formal patterning on skyscrapers, and a fixed ratio between plot size and tower footprint, rather than restricting height per se. From the top floor observatory of hindsight we can see the evolution of the set-back design of New York and then Chicago skyscrapers not as a response to the problem of human air rights, but as the unconscious construction of a staircase fit for King Kong. True, the giant ape swarms up the façade of the Empire State, yet once he nears the top he is able to hold Ann Darrow out in front of him, all the better to perform his snuffling inter-specific *totenlieder*. In my memory Kong is always enormous, fully the equal of the manmade peak he scales. Still, every time I review the scene I am shocked by how he is dwarfed by the Empire State Building far more than Ann Darrow is by him. Kong is us—or, rather, Kong is the prototypical superhuman of twentieth-century myth, and at least fleetingly the skyline of Manhattan is his jungle gym.

Kong is thus the wayfinder for all the bat-, super-, iron- and plastic men that will follow on behind; each of whom is, in their various ways, attempting to re-apprehend the intelligible with their magically enhanced sensibilities. Indeed, flipping through back issues of Marvel and DC comics it is impossible to avoid the conclusion that the entire genre exists largely as an unconscious response to the skyscraper.

Frame after frame features these limber figures leap-
ing, back-flipping and curvetting over row after row
of Mies van der Rohe; that Kong himself was a per-
sonification of the re-insemination of the machine
age by the primitive necessitates his own penetration
by .50 caliber machine gun bullets synchronized
to fire through diaphanous airplane propellers. He
falls—or perhaps jumps—and takes with him the
edenic and irenic reverie of a city that can still be
enjoyed haptically rather than visually. The superhe-
roes that succeed him are the humans we wish we
were; whereas the lowly apes that grub-up the news
in the offices of the *Daily Planet* or knuckle-walk
along the slot canyons of Gotham are condemned to
an unthinking and bestial existence in a built environment over which they can exert no management,
let alone control.

Like a window cleaner's cradle dangling from a
davit in high wind, American popular culture can't
help letting it all hang out. The recrudescence of the
Athenian polis in the spatialization of the Manhattan
skyline—a solid block of concrete, steel and masonry
neatly sliced into democratically accountable chunks—
brought with it the original Grecian sin: hubris. The
supercharged sexual lucubrations of Ayn Rand's
Atlas Shrugged are entirely besides the point here—
"It was like a phallic symbol ..." Tom Waits groans
about the Empire State Building in the song "King
Kong," but as I think we've already established,
there's no need to stretch to similitude. As the fuse
cupboards explode and flames wasp-waist the
135-story tower, Doug Roberts, the architect played by
Paul Newman asks Fire Chief Mike O'Hallorhan—
mummed by Steve McQueen—"Just how bad is it?"
To which O'Hallorhan replies: "Depends how
good your imagination is." The answer is, of course,

not terribly good at all–because it doesn't need to be. The so-called Master of Disaster, Irwin Allen, ushered in the counterweight to all those Lycra-clad leapers with *The Towering Inferno* (1974), a film whose release lagged only a few months behind the completion of the World Trade Center.

Corrupt developers and their senatorial shills mill around in the Promenade Room; their celebratory party has been abandoned and now they must fight to gain access to the scenic lifts scooting down the glassy flanks of the world's tallest skyscraper. With blue-collar probity etched into every angle of his face, Chief O'Hallorhan sneers, "Architects!" To which smooth Doug Roberts can only rejoin, "Yeah, it's all our fault." Over the next three decades, and now on into the new century, the bonfire of the vanities has never wanted for more fuel; the raising of one actual skyscraper is effectively twinned with the destruction of its cinematic doppelganger. J. G. Ballard's 1981 novel *Hello America*, features an expedition mounted from Europe in 2114 to visit the ecologically ravaged remains of the former superpower; and which redis-covers the skyscrapers of Manhattan sticking out, like the bones of a dinosaur, from 100-foot-high sand dunes. Ballard's fervid skill in conjuring up the sen-sation of silica on silicate was about to be eclipsed; indeed, if the medium is CGI its message is "Get a kick out of those two vast and trunkless legs." Best case is that the rapacious appetite Hollywood imag-ineers display for deluging, flaming, death-raying, exploding, and otherwise laying waste to the central business districts of American cities is an ironic com-ment on the short specs of some of their signature skyscrapers. But irony isn't Hollywood's major key.

No, whereas in *The Towering Inferno* there are only close-ups, mid- and long-shots, the mastery of

the disaster consists in their effective harmonization;
with the advent of CGI it becomes possible–at
least in theory–for disbelief to remain suspended high
above the skyscrapers, an all-seeing eye that
contemplates *The Day after Tomorrow* for its entire
nauseating duration. But by creating the super-
viewer–taller, faster, and stronger than a collapsing
skyscraper–the imagineers have simply reconfigured
the problem at a different scale; now we are too
big to experience our cities' destruction feelingly,
just as before we were too small to inhabit them
empathetically: Lunch(ing) atop a Skyscraper, we
were, each of us with his baloney sub in waxed
paper and his soda bottle, part of a Renaissance
group reclining on a girder, one that wouldn't have
been any more or less comfortable were that girder
to have been lain on the ground in front of a half-
built basilica. And surely, that was the entire point
of what was intended to be a publicity shot for the
RCA Building, a skyscraper that was completed in
the same year *King Kong* was released.

If Hollywood doesn't mete out brimstone to go
with the fire it rains down on the hubristic sinners
of Babel, it's only because Smell-o-Vision never
caught on. It is certainly not to do with any restraint
on their part. Following the destruction of the Twin
Towers by Al Qa'eda-backed terrorists in 2001 you
might have expected some compunction about the
vivid portrayal of skyscrapers being destroyed. Not
a bit of it–if anything, the frequency of their cinematic annihilation has only increased as competing
teams of visualizers do battle with one another for
the wilting credulity of the viewers. How could it be
otherwise, when the phenomenon itself is so devoid
of manifest content, but only responding to a brute
fact: the number of mega-structures going up keeps

on … going up. I say free of manifest content, yet
what I really want to say is that the willed destruction of the Twin Towers by religious fanatics steeped
in Judeo-Christian eschatology made this latent content so very manifest that the myth became a tale the
telling of which was effectively over. After 9/11, in a
very important sense, the skyscraper simply ceased
to exist. Just as my teenagers defend their first-per-
son-shooting of virtualized Nazi zombies on the
grounds that "They're Nazis *and* they're zombies," so
the zombie skyscrapers continue to stalk the globe,
only their *raison d'être* dispersed through the cloud
of toxic dust that billowed out from lower Manhattan
throughout that endless and apocalyptic day.

How to show the storied skyline after 9/11
became a problem for the visualizers. Steven
Spielberg ended his slick amorality fable, *Munich*, by
having one of his Mossad assassins cast a monitory
glance over his shoulder at the Twin Towers, but a
film director this accomplished should have known
that prolepsis—the film is set in the late 1970s—
can never compel catharsis; after all, how can anyone feel better about the state-sanctioned murders
deemed necessary revenge for crimes that have yet
to happen? The release in 2008 of James Marsh's
Man on Wire, a feature-length documentary about
Philippe Petit's 1974 guerrilla high-wire walk
between the Twin Towers, was a cause not for the
celebration of the indomitable human spirit—which
would, anyway, have been another prolepsis—but
for a faux-reconnection with an earlier and more
naïve age, one when it was possible for gang of ren-
egade circus artists to breach security without too
much trouble, all in the cause of a spectacle whimsi-
cal rather than world-shattering. Pertinently, the
wire walk remained unfilmed, so it disappeared into

a still more profound lacuna than the towers themselves, while Petit, interviewed on camera, had the definite feel of a man who had surpassed his wildest expectations while still in his relative infancy. He may have kept his footing on the wire, but for the rest of his life he was in free fall.

How could it be otherwise? This was a stupendous feat of bravery and conquest; Petit himself became during the hour-long walk—throughout which he frolicked and struck attitudes—a real life Superman, apprehending the skyscrapers directly through his own twanging form. That he subsequently found himself unable to comment on the destruction of the World Trade Center (which Marsh's film also makes no mention of), is a pure and Coleridgian involute: the buildings that he had so romantically linked had ceased to exist, not simply now, but in 1974 as well. This is also why the presence in the opening sequence of *The Sopranos* of the Twin Towers, which are glimpsed over Tony Soprano's shoulder as he exits the Lincoln Tunnel en route to his mafia fiefdom of North Jersey, seems quite so *unheimlich*: in the face of the painful verisimilitude of the series—which inaugurated a renaissance in American television drama that endures to this day—it is the World Trade Center that confirms its true status as pure fiction. The same might be said of the opening sequence of *Mad Men*, another lavishly produced series that, in the manner of Balzac's *Comédie humaine* attempts to link together, through drama, the unravelling strands of American culture and society in the decades following the Second World War.

This sequence uses spare graphics of the style employed by the "mad men" of the title (a self-ascription of cynically self-congratulatory Madison

Avenue advertising executives of the 1950s and '60s) to show a white-shirted, dark-suited man plunging downwards in mute supplication—arms outstretched, legs akimbo—past the cubism of sparsely-limned sky-scrapers. Although strenuously denied by its creators, this forces on the informed viewer's mind, quite unavoidably, the image of the so-called jumpers, those most benighted individuals, who, facing either immolation in the fires raging after the hijacked planes smashed into the North and South Towers, or certain—but possibly less painful—death upon impact with the ground, chose to fling themselves from the upper floors. In particular the *Mad Men* sequence recalls the most famous image of them: the "Falling Man," a shot of a still-unidentified man plunging from the North Tower, taken by the veteran AP photographer Richard Drew. Head down, arms at his sides, legs half-bent as if in the act of walking within the blurring lines of the skyscraper's graticule, the Falling Man became the focus of intense specu-lation—and even theorizing—in the months and then years after the terrorist attack. His apparent Petit-like insouciance in the face of death—and by extension his domination of the built environment that was an accessory to his (self) murder—was of course, just that: a trick of the lens.

For some the unsettling, willing-victim feel of the Falling Man became just another reason to airbrush out of history those who had jumped from the Twin Towers. The NYC Medical Examiner's Office is on record as stating that it does not consider those who fell from the World Trade Center to be "jumpers" as ordinarily understood—for this implies the premed-itation of a commonplace (!) suicide. Still, setting intentionality to one side for the moment, it is easy to see that the jumpers are a complete confirmation of the submerged but still dominant mythos of the Western skyscraper. In *The Towering Inferno* the adulterous businessman is immolated—the first actual death we witness on screen—as he tries futilely to find a way out of the conflagration for him and his lover; shortly after this, the woman taken in sin jumps from the skyscraper. That the people killed in the Twin Towers were a believably representative sample of the world's population, while the buildings they worked in were, in turn, credible icons of transnational capital flows, only serves to complete the apotheosis:

> Go to, let us go down, and there confound their language, that they may not understand one another's speech. So the Lord scattered them abroad from thence upon the face of all the earth: and they left off to build the city.

In the years since the violent opponents of usury (a prohibition contemporary Salafist jihadis share with Medieval Christians) launched their attack on the Babel-that-was-Mammon, the skyscraper has struggled to maintain any salience at all. In 2008, on a two-day hike across the auto-plutocratic city-state of Dubai and into the Empty Quarter of Arabia, I marveled at skyscraper after skyscraper, built by indentured labor, and each seemingly a more bowdlerized example of that inherently bowdlerizing architectural style, postmodernism. Hypertrophied mansard roofs supported by gargantuan Corinthian columns; Pantagruelian porticos leaning out over six-lane expressways planted with wastes of begonias drenched in costly desalinated water—the spectacle Dubai presents is of a last-chance saloon at which all the formal decadences of the West have come home to die. And then there's the matter of scale: by elevating detailing more suited to a sports shoe or an SUV thousands of feet into the sky, the Dubai skyscrapers themselves apotheosize those first Manhattan up-thrusts, whereby the Belle Époque was blasted into inner-space. Now, the new International Style is that of the desktop toy or bibelot writ horribly large.

Here in my hometown of London it isn't only the Shard that instantiates in the skyscraper a tendency the English architectural critic Owen Hatherley has noted: the elision of icon and logo in a single structure. The nicknames for these vast promotional devices follow ineluctably: "the Walkie-Talkie," and "the Cheesegrater" have joined the Gherkin and the Shard itself in altering for the foreseeable future the skyline of the city and the perspectives it enjoins on its traditionally earthborn inhabitants; we await with mild trepidation "the Quill" and some 200 others. And while there may be desultory coverage of these pharaonic undertakings—in and of themselves joshing the much-loved Skyscraper Index, since the country as a whole continues to hover above the oubliette of recession—the popular and collective apprehension of them is more or less nonexistent; apart, that is, from the *Private Eye* Lookalikes squib.

It was said of J. R. R. Tolkien that while a devout Catholic himself, he labored carefully to expunge the Judeo-Christian worldview from *The Lord of the Rings*, putting in its place what he saw as an older and deeper moral eschatology. That may well be; and it may also be true that the Two Towers of Isengard and Barad-dur (the Dark Tower) were inspired by a pair of particularly ugly Victorian water towers close to his boyhood home in Birmingham. Still, the

meticulous scholar of Anglo-Saxon—and wild fanta-
sist—nonetheless managed to zero-in on the popular
cultural consciousness of the twenty-first century
with uncanny prescience.

Shortly before I sat down to write this essay the
latest in a whole series of Arab mega-structures was
completed. Largely ignored in the West—which, as
you recall, has no need even of a bad imagination—
these include the crazed bodkin of the Kingdom
Centre in Riyadh, and of course the Burj Khalifa in
Dubai. In the next two decades even this uppermost
peak is set to be overtopped by at least ten more
vast skyscrapers in the region; but the Abraj Al-Bait
Towers in Mecca are undoubtedly the purest expression of the deep correspondence between the Shard
and Isengard. An engorged hulk of pseudo-Neo-
classicism only eleven meters shorter than the Burj
Khalifa, the Towers do indeed tower over the Masjid
al-Haram and its meteoric core, the Kaaba. Many of
the 3,000 hotel rooms and suites in the seven towers
that make up this manmade massif are positioned so
that their windows look right down into the holy-of-
holies, so encouraging devotion in their temporary
tenants. But it is the giant clock set in the Mecca
Royal Clock Tower forming Abraj Al-Bait's summit
that cements together those two seemingly disparate
lookalikes, the Shard and Isengard. Underneath the
iconic logo of the horned moon sit four clock faces,
each six feet larger in diameter than London's Big
Ben, and bearing a distinct resemblance to that most
imperialist of timepieces.

Mohammed al-Arkubi, general manager of the
hotel, is reported as saying that "Putting Mecca time
in the face of Greenwich Mean Time, this is the
goal." It's a fruitless goal if he expects the inhabitants
of Middle Earth—sorry, I mean the West—to pay any

attention. We don't so much as look upon our own tower of Isengard, whose designer's stated aim it was to create a skyscraper that disappeared vaporously into the surrounding atmosphere—and we know better than to even glance at the compound eye of Sauron that floats atop the Dark Tower of Barad-dur (sorry, I mean Abraj Al-Bait). And if you were tell us that this sky-scraping nemesis, like so many of the Arabian towers, had been built by the Saudi Binladen Group, why, we'd only shrug our shoulders and observe, Why not? After all, they are the biggest construction company in the world.

Buildings Are Not Supposed to Move

Emily Badger

The night Hurricane Alicia struck Houston in the summer of 1983, shattering high-rise windows downtown and stacking sailboats in the marina, there were two engineers waiting on the top floor of the Allied Bank Plaza. The seventy-one-story emerald glass tower–since renamed, and renamed again–had just opened that year. In August, its top floor was still unfinished. Unconnected wires dangled from the ceiling.

The engineers had driven in the middle of the night through rising gales and past sandbagged garages. A maintenance worker inside the building, on lockdown for the storm, had to operate the elevator for them. It wobbled on the way to the sky lobby, where the floor was already swaying noticeably, and then to the top, where the maintenance worker had the good sense to promptly return to the ground floor.

Robert Halvorson and Michael Fletcher made the trip to switch on equipment they had rented that would measure how the wind would play with the building, batting it back and forth along both axes and twisting it around its core. Then, they stayed for several hours–past the point when they could no longer walk upright, well beyond the moment when they realized they could see flickering lights in the distance coming in and out of view as the tower contorted.

I had been told about this building, in this storm, by several people preoccupied with the study of skyscrapers in wind. In their world, where such live experiments are rare, and where human reaction in the midst of motion is variable and tricky to measure, the Allied Bank Plaza in 1983 stands out as a singular event: structural engineers were actually present, bearing accelerometers and their own senses.

I asked Halvorson what the motion on the seventy-first floor felt like in the middle of a storm that ended up devastating the city. "The only thing that was on your mind," he recalled, "was moving around. There was no other thing that was of interest, no other thing you could do."

The floor seemed to shift beneath him and Fletcher unpredictably. The wind pushed and pulled on the windowpanes, turning the glass into funhouse mirrors reflecting distorted images of the men inside.

Even at the height of the hurricane, the Allied Bank Plaza was never in structural danger, a reality the engineers were confident of in the back of their minds. What buildings can tolerate, however, is very different from what their humans can. We get motion sickness. We lose concentration. We are overcome by fear.

Engineers and architects could create perfectly stable, structurally sound skyscrapers that safely sway more than we even allow them to. But the human body responds violently to rhythmic motion. And, even at much subtler levels, our minds don't handle it well, either. As sure as Halvorson was that the Allied Bank Plaza would not tip over, most of us harbor an opposing notion: *buildings are not supposed to move.*

It is this conviction, as much as any law of physics, that constrains and shapes the design of skyscrapers we're now pursuing even higher into the wind.

In fact, all buildings move. This truth, which physics must tell us because human perception cannot, renders clear two humbling points: much of the world is not as solid as we think, and humans are awfully poor receptors.

The Pentagon moves. Madison Square Garden moves. Even the Pyramids move. Perhaps only on a miniscule scale and during the most severe windstorms, but every material and structural system must deform under its load. Nothing, according to physics, can be infinitely rigid. But as we have succeeded in building taller, narrower, and lighter, the acceleration of movement at the top of a building—under just the right circumstances swinging to one side, then to the center, to the other side, and back again—has eclipsed the threshold of conscious human perception.

Architects and engineers knew this in the 1930s. The engineer David Cushman Coyle was dragging a device of his own invention then to the tops of New York's skyscrapers, measuring the motion that was giving people "sky sickness." In a 1938 issue of *Popular Science Monthly*, Coyle appears bending over his suitcase-sized contraption under a lyric headline: "New machine proves skyscrapers shiver in wind." In the thirties, Coyle warned that the frames of tall buildings had to be stiff enough to keep the vibration caused by wind "within limits that inspire occupants with confidence in the strength of the structure."

In the earliest days of the Chrysler and the Empire State buildings, engineers understood that it wasn't enough to design for structural integrity; they had to design for the even narrower parameters of human confidence. What they did not know then—and what they are still learning now—is exactly where those bounds lie.

The physics of motion are the simple part, dictated by equations (force equals mass times acceleration) and measured in known quantities (thousandths of gravity). The worst problems arise not from wind striking the face of a building, but from wind traveling along it. Picture how water moves past a rowboat, creating swirling eddies in the boat's wake. Wind does something very similar as it courses around the edge of a tower, shedding spinning vortices as it goes.

These vortices, invisible little tornadoes, peel off along one side of the building, then the other, in alternating patterns that during strong winds can set an entire skyscraper vibrating. Here, another analogy is in order: buildings are also a bit like tuning forks. Strike a tuning fork, and it vibrates at its natural frequency, producing an audible pitch. Buildings have natural frequencies as well, although their vibrations occur at much slower speeds than a tuning fork. Your ear cannot hear them.

Skyscrapers really start to rock when the vibrations caused by vortex shedding bring the building's motion into harmony with its natural frequency. One last analogy, which is popular among structural engineers when they're forced to explain all of this to laymen: imagine a small child on a swing set. She's kicking her feet—not a very impressive display of power. But if she does this with just the right rhythm, the swing rises higher and higher. It may take some time to get the thing going, but once she does, it takes little effort to maintain the motion. This is how the seemingly outmatched force of moving air along a planar surface, gusting over a sustained period of time, can get a 500,000-ton steel-and-concrete skyscraper rocking back and forth.

Inside the building, on those top floors, the oscillation is what unnerves us. A forty-story building may sway a foot to the left, a foot to the right. The span of that period might last around four seconds. A hundred-story building, by comparison, may move on the order of two-and-a-half to three feet to each side, cycling through a ten-second period. Typically, the taller the building, the longer the period of its cyclical motion.

Sitting in a penthouse living room, the displacement of two or three feet would be imperceptible to you. "You would be like a fly on an elephant," says Nick Isyumov, a retired professor of civil and environmental engineering at the University of Western Ontario. "The elephant would be moving, and the fly wouldn't care." Humans are also terrible at perceiving velocity at a constant speed. This is why, when you're traveling on a train at a steady fifty miles an hour, your body believes you might as well be sitting perfectly still. What we can feel, however, is acceleration—a train, or a building, *gaining* speed as it moves.

Acceleration is what causes the body forces that might tip us off our firmly planted feet, or nudge us back into the passenger seat of a car pulling away from a stoplight. Fighter pilots experience acceleration at many times the magnitude of gravity—"4 Gs" or more. The top of our hundred-story skyscraper accelerates through its period, as it sways from one side to the other, at a mere fraction of what a fighter pilot feels: maybe ten milli-g's, or one hundredth of the force of gravity.

At that acceleration, most people would be able to perceive some sense of motion. Recognizing this, engineering standards for buildings in North America for the last thirty years have recommended that the top occupied floor of residential towers not accelerate beyond fifteen-to-eighteen milli-g's during the kind of storm that is likely to occur once every ten years. The criteria are more lax for commercial buildings—twenty-to-twenty-five milli-g's—on the grounds that it's easier to evacuate an office than an apartment during an extraordinary storm like Alicia. It is also arguably less alarming when such motion occurs while you're seated at a desk than when you're leaning over your kitchen stove, trying to spoon marinara to your mouth.

That night in the Allied Bank Plaza in 1983—when, as planned, all of the commercial buildings downtown were evacuated—Halvorson and Fletcher recorded a peak acceleration of forty-three milli-g's.

"Now," says Bill Baker, the chief structural engineer at Skidmore, Owings & Merrill, who, along with Isyumov, patiently clarified much of this for me, "having said that, a lot of the perception of motion is not related to this thing that we can calculate."

Buildings are much easier to assess than humans beings. Where they are measurable and predictable, we are variable and illogical. One person may perceive the faintest tremors of an earthquake, while another may never know that one passed. The rise and fall of a sailboat that makes one man seasick may feel unremarkable to his co-captain. Even more confounding: in "moving room" experiments, conducted by Melissa Burton as part of her Ph.D. studies at the Hong Kong University of Science and Technology, nearly one in five people who were never subjected to motion at all believed that they had been when the question was later asked of them.

Our perception of motion sits at the messy confluence of physiology and psychology. Much of the understanding of it originally came from fields far outside of architecture, from the study of people aboard ships or piloting airplanes. In the early 1960s, a British engineer named E. G. Walsh first confirmed that our ability to sense motion derives from the vestibular apparatus in our inner ear. In experiments conducted at a school for deaf children, he asked subjects to lie down on a swinging stretcher suspended between four wires, which he gradually rocked back and forth. Compared to other subjects, children with a damaged vestibular apparatus perceived only the more dramatic motion.

Today, researchers believe that the most sensitive people, about ten percent of the population, begin to perceive motion around three or four milli-g's. Discomfort starts to sets in between ten and twenty milli-g's. When we feel this kind of back-and-forth movement at periods of between three and six seconds, we become particularly susceptible to nausea. Then, as acceleration continues to rise, we have trouble manipulating utensils, and managing hand- and foot-to-eye coordination. At around forty milli-g's, walking becomes difficult, and above that, we struggle to maintain our balance. Somewhere around forty-five milli-g's—roughly the level Halvorson and Fletcher experienced—debilitating fear kicks in for most of us.

These numbers, though, represent shades of perception, not the hard math of engineering. And beyond the onset of nausea, or the difficulty maintaining balance—both physiological reactions—so much of motion perception has little to do with the actual workings of the inner ear. In an apartment at the top of a skyscraper, we are also susceptible to cues outside of our bodies: to the sight of a chandelier swinging or water sloshing in a toilet bowl, to the sound of elevator cables clanging or the creaking of a building's structural frame. "You may perceive that a whole lot earlier than your inner ear feels the motion," Baker says. And these other cues may be just as disturbing.

Even in sophisticated moving-room studies, where a room-sized box is placed atop hydraulics capable of simulating the precise motion of building sway, it's impossible to recreate the fear we bring with us to the top of skyscrapers, or the shock we experience when movement interrupts our domestic routines. It's impossible to simulate the cognitive dissonance of standing in a moving building that you believe is not supposed to move.

All of this context is essential to understanding why small motions that would not have much impact in other settings deeply trouble us at a hundred stories. "Ultimately, it is the uncertainty that is really the principle," Isyumov tells me. We don't know if the building might tip over, or if it's supposed to behave this way, or when such motion might strike again. "We have this built-in mentality that some things move—like cars and elevators and airplanes," Isyumov says. "And other things do not, such as buildings."

Americans are particularly wedded to this conviction. Our litigiousness, Burton says, makes us less tolerant of building motion than people she has studied in other parts of the world, suggesting that there is also a cultural component to how we perceive movement. Other research suggests that personality matters, too. People who are more neurotic tend to complain about motion at levels that don't bother the rest of us.

In theory, some of the fear associated with motion might ease with repeated exposure and education. Air traffic controllers, for instance, learn to concentrate while experiencing the sway of their traffic control towers. Likewise, tall building occupants might learn to shrug off minor motion if they could appreciate that some movement is inevitable, even natural, in any built system. But habituation solves only the psychological elements of motion perception, not the physiological ones. Those we cannot accustom ourselves to. "Motion sickness is like this evil sickness that humans suffer from," Burton says, "and we're stuck with it."

Fundamentally, though, the distinction between the physiological and the psychological is unimportant. Did you really *feel* a building move? Or do you *believe* you felt it move because you saw the chandelier sway? "Ultimately, it doesn't matter to us as the engineer or the designer," Burton says. "Ultimately, what matters is if it's being perceived at all."

In North America, the rules for acceptable building motion are based on a cruder product of these interrelated psychological and physiological variables: at what point are people inside a moving building likely to complain about it? The fifteen to eighteen milli-g standard is derived from that deeply pragmatic threshold, the point at which past experience suggests the most sensitive two percent of residents in the top third of a building will complain about the motion experienced during a typical ten-year storm.

The small size of that hypersensitive population, during a rare, hypothetical event, might appear insignificant, particularly given its outsize influence on the design and engineering of an entire skyscraper. But given the high stakes of building high—for property managers, owners, engineers, and architects—the complaints of a few may be enough to seed broader fears that a building is unsound.

This is where skyscrapers pile one final, absurd demand on engineers. The less a building moves—thanks to more robust structural systems—the more expensive it is to build. And so the engineer's task is to guide a building's blueprint into that narrow space between what is cost-prohibitive on a balance sheet and what is minutely perceptible to the human body. "OK, now I've solved for gravity, I've solved for basic strength and wind," says Chuck Besjak, the director of structural engineering at SOM. Now the engineer must solve for people.

There are blunt ways to do this, with dampers or massive building-top tanks in which hundreds of gallons of water slosh around, counteracting the sway of a tower in high winds. Or, as engineers poetically put it, they can design buildings, like the Burj Khalifa, where the form of the towers themselves contribute to "confusing the wind."

The 2,700-foot tower in Dubai grows more slender as it rises in an inverted Y-shape, with three wings buttressing its core—a shape that took form in a wind tunnel. Bill Baker and his colleagues kept tweaking and testing the geometry. They turned the building 120 degrees to account for Dubai's prevailing winds. They altered the direction of its signature setbacks, which now wrap around the tower as they ascend clockwise.

The final result may look like the product of an architect's ego, an elaborate minaret rising from the Arabian desert, but it is also a bulwark built to mock the wind. In the coming ten- or twenty-year storms, it will be exceptionally difficult for the kind of vortices to form off the Burj Khalifa that would cause the tower to vibrate forcefully.

Now, as the world's ever-taller supertalls aim to top the Burj, the tools available to simulate movement in wind, and shape towers to withstand it, are growing more sophisticated, more precise. They are a far cry from the homemade machine David Cushman Coyle used to prove that skyscrapers "shiver" in the wind. RWDI, a Canadian wind engineering consultant, can rapid-prototype building models with a 3D printer, then monitor the dynamic response of those models a thousand ways in a wind tunnel. RWDI has even begun to work with a ship simulator at Memorial University in Newfoundland. The Centre for Marine Simulation there has more than a dozen simulators built to train seamen to manage a ship in violent seas. The top floor of the Chicago Spire was also simulated there, as was the penthouse of a 1,400-foot-tall residential tower at 432 Park Avenue in Manhattan.

In each case, the equipment in a simulator meant to model a ship's bridge was replaced–a couch was brought in, a table set for dinner, a chandelier. A skyscraper's view of the city replaced the simulator's views of the sea, all to give engineers and architects a sense of what the math in a wind tunnel might mean in the real world.

As skyscrapers grow taller, evolving with the tools that make such heights realistic, it's possible that we'll change, too. "We fly in airplanes, we have people going off to the moon," Isyumov says. "It makes absolutely no sense why we cannot educate the public that movement of buildings is in fact one of their characteristics, as long as that movement doesn't make you ill." Maybe when more of us live in skyscrapers, when 2,700 feet becomes an unremarkable height, ten milli-g's during a dinner party won't mean much to us anymore.

By then, engineers will know even more about how to confuse the wind, if not about the remaining mysteries of human perception. Their record, even in 1983, was impressive. Isyumov did the original wind tunnel testing on the Allied Bank Plaza.

"The one really startling, wonderful conclusion that came out of that," Halvorson says of his live experiment, "was that what we measured in the field was, give or take, exactly the same thing that had been predicted by the wind tunnel. Here's this little teeny building in this little teeny city, in a modest-size wind tunnel with some little gauges on it. And from playing around with that, they are able to predict more or less exactly how this building would behave."

And that was thirty years ago, before 3D printers and marine simulators, before wind tunnel sensors capable of taking measurements 500 times a second. "That's remarkable," Halvorson continues, "given all the variables of nature and construction, and the limits of our computer analysis."

If engineers can be so accurate with the modeling of buildings in motion, perhaps they can also come to discover what remains mysterious about their human occupants: the limits of fear and culture, perception and personality, body and mind.

A Singularity of Integrated Functions

Dickson Despommier

What is a city? Or, more to the point, *why* is a city? It is probable that most who live in cities or in their neighboring suburbs do not spend much time thinking about the origins of the built environment in which they live. It is even more likely that none of those same people contemplate what their city might look like in another fifty years. For many it is challenging enough in a crowded, modern metropolis just to navigate one's way to and from work each day. Those are no small triumphs in the constant struggles facing the urbanized fifty percent of the world—be they in New York City, Paris, Mumbai, Singapore, or Seoul. As if worrying about timely mobility were not enough to keep urbanites pointed in the right direction, over the last several hundred years, the city has stealthily morphed into a glitzy, neon-lit milieu enticing its denizens to choose from an extensive array of distractions: buy these, eat here, smoke me, drink this, sleep in our bed tonight, go to this play, and so on. And if the transit systems break down, the sanitation workers go on strike, or a megastorm floods the downtown section that just happens to include your two favorite eateries, it's a major catastrophe. But somehow we manage to plod on, focusing in on some insignificant thing, such as a sporting event, a cooking show, the latest gossip about so-and-so, and then we turn out the lights to do it all over again the next day. In short, most of us would agree that a fast-paced life leaves little room for philosophical debate, regardless of the importance of the subject.

Yet if we are to alter the developmental pathways of cities[1] to create sustainable urban

1   L. M. A. Bettencourt, "The Origins of Scaling in Cities," *Science* 340 (April 2013).

environments at the millennial level, and at the same time, address issues of ecosystem repair, then coming up with the correct answers to these two queries— *What is a city*? and *Why*?—are challenges that require immediate and positive responses. Time is not on the side of those who wish things to go on as they are, ignoring altogether the fate of the next generations. We have to come to grips with the process of inventing the city of the future, and reshape it into one that is fully compatible with the rest of the natural world. And we must do this while providing every citizen with a comfortable, healthy lifestyle filled with hope and promise. To fail in these related goals would mark the end of a world we have unwittingly created by our penchant for unregulated growth.

An Ecological Perspective
Within the last ten years, the rate of loss of natural systems has been accelerating at an ever-increasing rate. Scientists from nearly every discipline have collaborated to document irreversible negative changes in many places that, just a few years earlier, used to support balanced, functional, diverse combinations of plants and animals—places we have come to refer to as ecosystems. Assemblages of plants and animals do not just exist side by side. They gradually evolve into complex interdependent relationships: the defining feature of all functional ecosystems.[2] Interdependence is the basis for an ecosystem's ability to rebound from natural disaster, be it flood, fire, drought, or catastrophic earthquake. Resiliency is key to an ecosystem's long-term viability.[3] But it is also possible to exceed the limits of an

2   Eugene Odum and Gary Barret, *Fundamentals of Ecology* (Philadelphia, 1953).

ecosystem's ability to recover. Human activities such as mining, urbanization, and farming have systematically disengaged many of these associations, turning intact ecosystems into wastelands, sometimes within a matter of only a few years.[4]

Over the last half century, the field of ecology has matured as a science, and because of this, we have learned much regarding the mechanisms that life-forms on Earth have evolved to ensure their long-term survival. Maintaining a high level of biodiversity is the foremost mechanism that makes ecosystem resiliency possible.[5] In an ideal world, within each ecosystem, all living networks are connected and have evolved mutually dependent associations. This is true on no matter which twig or branch of the tree of life we begin our search for interdependencies. Resilient, thriving societal systems also appear to be governed by similar principles. The well-established field of industrial ecology[6] documents this human activity, the kind that was undoubtedly inspired by nature.[7] Incorporating the concepts of interconnectedness and diversity into the

3   Gene Likens and F. Herbert Bormann, *Biogeochemistry of a Forested Ecosystem* (New York, 1994), p. 164.

4   World Health Organization, "Ecosystem goods and services for health," http://www.who.int/globalchange/ecosystems/en/.

5   E. O. Wilson, *Diversity of Life: Questions of Science* (New York, 1999), p. 440.

6   William McDonough and Michael Braungart, *Cradle To Cradle: Remaking the Way We Make Things* (New York: 2002); Ray Anderson, *Business Lessons From a Radical Industrialist* (New York, 2009), p. 336; T. E. Graedel and Bradley R. Allenby, *Industrial Ecology* (Upper Saddle River, NJ, 2003), p. 363.

7   Janine M. Benyus, *Biomimicry: Innovation Inspired By Nature* (New York, 1997), p. 320.

fabric of a new city will enable it to prosper, even in lean times.

Unfortunately, not nearly enough information on how natural systems behave has filtered down to politicians and policy makers to make a difference in their ability to perceive global problems and to formulate and implement solutions to address them. Nonetheless, the vast majority of us are aware that at no other time in the history of our planet has one species (us) had such a dramatic and negative effect on all other life.[8]

One reason we continue to sacrifice natural systems for the built environment[9] is that we seriously undervalue the roles played by the natural world in helping us to "live long and prosper." It comes as no surprise that our relentless encroachment into countless ecosystems, mostly in the last two hundred years, has created numerous examples—clustering of cancers, increase in respiratory diseases, emergence of numerous infectious agents, to name a few[10]—with some of these health problems affecting everyone, regardless of geography. Our complete lack of sensitivity at the societal level regarding the importance of ecological relationships to our well-being has resulted in the extinction of countless species. By leveling entire swaths of tropical forests we have

8   E. C. Ellis, "Anthropogenic Transformation of the Terrestrial Biosphere," *Philosophical Transactions of the Royal Society of London* 369 (2011).

9   G. Bakla, et al., "Combined Climate and Carbon Cycle Effects of Large Scale Deforestation," *Proceedings of the National Academy of Sciences* 104 (April 2007).

10   Anthony J. McMichael and Colin D. Butler, "Emerging Health Issues: The Widening Challenge for Population Health Promotion," *Health Promotion International* 21 (December 2006).

destroyed ecological relationships that evolved over
millions of years.

The Rise of Cities:
A Very Brief Historical Overview

For generations scholars have struggled to define
how and why the concept of urban life evolved in
the first place.[11] Perhaps it began simply by humans
adhering to the old adage of survival: that there is
safety and strength in numbers. As more of us came
into the world, life has tended to get more and more
confrontational—witness the demise of Ötzi the
Ice Man, who suffered a violent death in the Austrian-
Italian Alps over 5,000 years ago.[12] Larger groups
may have, on average, prevailed through sheer
numbers and won the day. In fact, a great deal of
recorded history is dedicated to the detailed recount-
ing of the seemingly endless conflicts between
warring societies the world over. So getting bigger
meant greater community survivability[13]; bigger
groups have bigger needs that might have been best
served by learning how to stay put and defending a
single geographic site. Nearly all ancient cities had
walls or moats that defined lines of defense. Troy, for
example, has seen at least eight rebirths throughout
its long and storied past.[14] The reasons vary greatly
as to why there were so many iterations. Some were

11   Lewis Mumford, *The City in History: Its Origins, Its
     Transformations, and Its Prospects* (New York, 1961).

12   A. G. Nerlich, "New Evidence for Ötzi's Final Trauma," *Intensive
     Care Magazine* 35 (January, 2009).

13   Warder Clyde Allee, ed., *Principles of Animal Ecology* (Michigan,
     1949).

14   UNESCO, "Archaeological Site of Troy," whc.unesco.org/en/
     list/849.

destroyed by natural forces (earthquakes, fires), while others were leveled by warfare often initiated by competition for scarce resources. In each case, Troy's strategic location proved irresistible to those who still wanted to reside there, and rebuilding became synonymous with the spirit of that tragedy-prone ancient metropolis.

Perhaps some cities developed due to disparate groups of travelers settling for extended periods at the intersection of high volume trade routes or the places where strategic waterways merged with estuaries (today's port cities). Some cities were fostered by the invention of agriculture,[15] which eliminated the need for wandering the countryside in search of daily sustenance. Or some might have been determined by the discovery of a scarce resource such as drinking water. Jericho was built around an abundance of springs, for example.[16] Each of these scenarios could have, on their own, accounted for why we began to cluster our populations into collectives that rapidly grew into cities as we know them today.

In the beginning, cities spread out in all directions from their points of origin without much in the way of planning to guide them, following paths of least resistance marked by river banks, harbors, or the foothills of mountain ranges. Proximity to essential resources caused cities to grow along mostly naturalistic patterns. Regardless of location, as life in cities improved they became hubs for continued growth due to immigration, as well as from the increasing birthrates. At all times urban

15   M. Balter, "Seeking Agriculture's Ancient Roots," *Science* 316 (June 2007).

16   Jericho City, official city website, www.jericho-city.org/etemplate.php?id=15.

sprawl was a frequent result, until resources and essential municipal services were stretched to their limits. Then, not infrequently, epidemics of infectious diseases emerged,[17] marking cities simultaneously as places of promise and a danger to be avoided at all costs. Prolonged drought that outlasted the consumption of essential resources,[18] or floods that swept away all that was not tied down,[19] also accounted for their share of failed cities. Most of the highly settled ancient citadels could weather any one of these adverse conditions. But when more than one disaster struck at the same time, they were soon abandoned. In the cradle of modern western civilization, the Middle East, anthropologists blame persistent drought, and the attendant loss of arable land due to primitive agricultural practices, as the primary reasons for urban extinction—see: Ur, Nineveh, Babylon, Jericho, Memphis, Petra, and many others—in that fragile, arid, unforgiving part of the world. In the end, lack of sustainable sources for essential resources resulted in an urban equivalent of the "failure to thrive" syndrome that continues to plague vast numbers of impoverished children born into the less developed world.[20]

Eventually, as entire civilizations arose and matured, their modal behaviors became identified with their capital cities, each one evolving a unique

17   Daniel Defoe, *A Journal of the Plague Year* (London, 1722).

18   R. Acuna-Soto et al. "Drought, Epidemic Disease, and the Fall of Classic Period Cultures in Mesoamerica (AD 750–950)," *Medical Hypotheses* 65 (2005).

19   N. B. Grimm, et al. "Global Change and the Ecology of Cities," *Science* 319 (2008).

20   Jared Diamond, *Collapse: How Societies Choose to Fail or Succeed* (New York, 2011) p. 608.

urban "personality." This was particularly true for
those Western cultures with rich, robust written
languages, such as the Egyptians, Greeks, or Romans.
Sparta, Athens, Alexandria, Rome, and Rhodes all
had unique features that still conjure up images
of iconic cultural landmarks (in music, literature,
mathematics, art, architecture, etc.). Yet, despite the
myriad achievements of these remarkable cultures, all
of them failed the ultimate test: sustainability.

At the risk of trivializing mountains-worth of
scholarly studies on the subject of why these enor-
mously influential cultures came to ignominious ends,
in each case climate change was probably the most
important contributing factor in their descent and
decline.[21] Since almost every ancient city experienced the phenomenon of overpopulation, demand
for a decidedly more people-friendly infrastructure
ultimately arose, especially among the privileged
classes, giving way in some remarkable instances to
city planning, such as occurred in ancient Rome.[22]
Following the discovery of basic mathematical
principles,[23] engineering soon became established
as a reputable occupation that occupied a place
of high importance next to architecture and planning, as evidenced in the remains of cultures from
Egypt, Rome, Asia, South Asia, Mexico, Central
America, and Peru. Successful practitioners of these
interrelated careers dedicated their lives to the
improvement of urban life, and reshaped sprawling

21   A. S. Issar, "Climate Change and the History of the Middle East,"
     American Scientist 83 (March–April, 1995), p. 350.

22   O. F. Robinson, *Ancient Rome: City Planning and Administration*
     (New York, 1994).

23   Dirk J. Struik, *A Concise History of Mathematics* (New York, 1987)
     p. 219.

chaotic urban landscapes into logical arrangements of municipal functions. The development of reliable waste-disposal systems, drinking water schemes, and the partitioning of residential and business districts of urban centers began to deviate from earlier attempts to live and work helter-skelter on the land. Despite this transformative change in urban planning, as alluded to above, the vast majority of ancient cities succumbed to a relentlessly changing climate regime, as humanity attempted to deal with a warming period that followed one of the great ice ages of modern geological history.

The Modern Metropolis

At present, the great majority of municipalities that have 100,000 or more in population have incorporated all of the essential services needed for them to qualify as modern cities. These include reliable sources of energy, drinking water, food, an adequate public health system, a responsive mass transit network, public education, and the establishment of viable commercial, entertainment, recreational, and residential districts. For example, in the United States alone, as of 2012, there were some 300 cities that qualified as "modern" under this definition. Over fifty percent of the global population now lives within urbanized zones[24] that in surface area represent only three to four percent of the Earth's total landmass.[25] But living in a crowded, compact world still takes its toll on the surrounding environment—

24   E. Kalnay and M. Cai, "Impact of Urbanization and Land-use Change on Climate," *Letters to Nature: Nature* 423 (2003), pp. 528–31.

25   Schneider A. Friedl, M. A. and Potere, D., "A New Map of Global Urban Extent from MODIS Satellite Data," *Environmental Research Letters* Vol. 4 (2009).

a phenomenon known as the *ecological* footprint.[26]
Land needed to supply everyone who lives in cities
with a reliable food supply now exceeds half the size
of South America, but that estimate only includes
the area required to grow edible plants. If we add
grazing land to the equation, then humans are now
farming nearly every available acre that can support
some form of agriculture.[27]

These statistics were derived from LandSat
satellite data beginning in 1972 and continuing to
the present with the recent launching of LandSat 8.
The program is specifically tied to the linked crises of
sub-optimal land-use and progressive climate change.
Using a suite of state-of-the-art instruments called
reflectometers, LandSat 8 can identify any naturally
occurring major plant species and most varieties
of planted crops. It can determine the age of the
crop, and whether or not it is growing optimally.
Thus, from outer space, we can obtain an exquisitely
detailed picture throughout the year as to what
kind of yields farmers can expect, regardless of where
their farms are located.[28] These data will undoubtedly result in a deeper understanding of our
penchant for using virtually every inch of space to
support agricultural initiatives ranging from traditional soil-based crop production to intensive
grazing. Future planning policies on land use will
benefit greatly from these insights. Perhaps when
these images, illustrating so well how we have

26   Mathis Wackernagel and William Rees, *Our Ecological Footprint:
      Reducing Human Impact on the Earth* (British Columbia, 1996).

27   Nicola, "Sixty-Six Percent Natural," *Edible Geography*, May 14,
      2010, www.ediblegeography.com/sixty-six-percent-natural/.

28   NASA, "Landsat 8: Landsat Overview," http://www.nasa.gov/
      mission_pages/landsat/overview/index.html#.UdB2rOuklls.

proceeded to engage the land to meet our caloric needs, become clear to the vast majority of humanity, we can then begin the process of redesigning not only our agricultural systems, but everything else associated with the basics of living on Earth, particularly how we manage the urban environment.

Over the next fifty years, it is expected that there will be another three billion people to feed. To do so will require an additional amount of farmland equivalent to the size of Brazil.[29] Unfortunately, there is no available arable land of that magnitude on Earth that is not already being farmed. This represents a problem so complex in scale that failure to address it now will make solutions increasingly difficult, and more and more driven by crisis. We must begin now to put together reasonable, achievable goals that will address this immense and looming problem, eventually achieving the result of a more equitable world with respect to resource management. At the same time, we must allow for the repair and recovery of damaged portions of the natural world. The best way to do that is just to leave nature alone; unburdened by human pressures, it will restore itself, often in rapid fashion.[30]

Managing the built environment as a "living" entity, composed of a series of interdependent, essential municipal services, maximizes the efficient use of limited resources (e.g., energy, water, land), and emulates the best features of functional ecosystems, systems that manage essential resources, irrespective of how abundant or scarce a given resource might be over the short term. Since resiliency is key to an

29   Population Council, www.popcouncil.org.

30   Holly P. Jones and Oswald J. Schmitz, "Rapid Recovery of Damaged Ecosystems," *PLoS One* 4(5): e5653 (May 27, 2009).

ecosystem's survival, there is no technical barrier thatwould exclude this behavior from a new city, if imagined and implemented as an ecosystem, as well. Yet very few governing bodies adhere to this principle of resiliency, largely because, in my view, they lack specific knowledge about the inner workings of natural systems. Rather, most large cities are politically structured along traditional late nineteenth- and early twentieth-century models, in which separate departments are responsible for providing each municipal service. Each commissioner, then, is in competition with all the others when it comes to providing adequate financial support for the growth and maintenance of his or her own systems. For example, the city of New York lists thirty-five individual commissioners for categories as widely diverse as sanitation, housing, corrections, park services, and education.[31] It might go without saying that the sharing of limited resources and a culture of interdepartmental collaboration are not encouraged by this kind of balkanized political structure.

In contrast, natural systems are entirely dependent for long-term survival upon cooperative (i.e., altruistic) behavior among their diverse assemblages of plants, animals, and microbes.[32] Witness the evolutionary success of the cell, tissues, organs, whole organisms, and a wide variety of disparate life forms, all of which share one keystone feature: their genetic material, DNA.[33] A common, carbon-based chemistry enables all life on earth to relate to one another using shared pathways. Built into these chemically complex but functionally related systems

31   City of New York, official city website, www.nyc.gov.

32   Robert L. Trivers, "The Evolution of Reciprocal Altruism," *The Quarterly Review of Biology* 46 (March 1971).

is an ordered series of genetically regulated redundancies and repair mechanisms that will not allow for the failure of a single essential cellular function.[34] Back-up systems have evolved to ensure that new cells can be generated for the purpose of forming whole organisms, or to replace those cells already produced that have become damaged or even killed by trauma or infection. In some areas of modern life we have learned from this organic example; we design commercial aircraft, for instance, to behave similarly, with backup systems in place to kick into action instantly in the event of a mechanical failure.[35]

The new city must evolve towards these goals as well, restructuring itself from an archaic collection of municipal fiefdoms into a singularity of integrated functions. Municipal redundancy/resiliency means never having to suffer catastrophic losses when natural disasters temporarily disrupt essential operations—such as public transportation, commerce, or the flow of energy, food or water. By taking advantage of a systems approach to the integration of technologies developed to address each of these now-separate urban functions, better-adapted cities of the future can be created, inspired by nature to protect the general well-being of each and every member of the collective urban community.

33   J. D. Watson and F. H. C. Crick, "Molecular Structure of Nucleic Acids: A Structure for Deoxyribose Nucleic Acid," *Nature* 171 (April 1953).

34   G. Dover, "Evolution of Genetic Redundancy for Advanced Players," *Current Opinion in Genetics & Development* 3, vol. 6 (1993).

35   E. Chow and A. S. Willsky, "Analytical Redundancy and the Design of Robust Failure Detection Systems," *IEEE Transactions* 29 (July 1984).

The New City:
More Than the Sum of Its Parts

Enabling a large city to adopt cost-effective, easy-to-maintain, and reliable interdependent municipal services will probably require a nearly complete remake of the urban landscape, employing heaps of creative re-engineering and difficult to obtain buy-ins from all segments of city government—as well as from, of course, its citizens. As daunting a task as this may at first seem, the good news is that much of what I propose is already deployed and in use some-where in the world today. So to expect that disparate engineering marvels such as the complete recovery and re-use of gray water,[36] effective zero landfill waste practices, on site production of bio-fuels for all municipal vehicles,[37] or even urban food produc-tion[38] could be applied all at the same time to our vision of the new city is not as unrealistic (or even as grandiose) at it may seem. In fact, the only thing now lacking in our plan to create an ecologically-inspired urban landscape is a significant increase in the amount of primary productivity: in other words, cities that can grow their own food.

Producing food inside the city takes the pres-sure off of the surrounding landscape. Thus, urban agriculture is the mechanism that allows for the res-toration of damaged ecosystems by allowing for the abandonment of rural farmland. It is estimated that for every indoor acre intensively farmed, ten outdoor

---

36   Lia Fangyue, Knut Wichmann and Ralf Otterpohl, "Review of the Technological Approaches for Grey Water Treatment and Reuses," *Science of the Total Environment* 407 (March 2009).

37   Linkoping, Sweden, official city website, www.linköpingcity.se.

38   Dickson Despommier, *The Vertical Farm: Feeding the World in the 21st Century and Beyond* (New York, 2010).

acres of land could be allowed to grow back into hardwood forest—since indoor farming is more efficient, does not suffer from crops lost due to weather events, and can be carried out under controlled conditions year round. If all of the world's cities were to produce just ten percent of what they now consume, an estimated 340,000 square miles of hardwood forest could be restored. To give some idea as to the amount of forest involved in this scheme, from 1970 to the present, Brazil has deforested some 600,000 square miles of tropical rainforest, converting it mostly into farmland.[39]

Vertical Farming:
Food Production Within the City
The vertical farm is the keystone enterprise for establishing any urban-based ecosystem. Without food production, no city can emulate the virtues of a functional, intact ecosystem: Bioproductivity is key for both. It is the defining mechanism for energy management for all living organisms. Yet, if the city can supply itself with at least fifty to eighty percent of its agricultural needs, then lots of other sustainable activities become achievable, allowing its citizens to capture and reuse the energy of their own metabolic byproducts and reclaim the grey water. Establishing vertical farming on a large scale would be the start to a complete remake of urban behavior centered around the concept of doing no harm to the environment.

In addition to restoring abundant areas of rainforest, hardwood forest, and ailing farmland while feeding a growing urban population, the vertical farm has many additional advantages. And they are advantageous to

39   Michael Williams, *Deforesting the Earth: From Prehistory to Global Crisis* (Chicago, 2006).

more than just the climate. There are health and safety, economic, and employment benefits as well:

1   Year-round crop production

2   No weather-related crop failures

3   No agricultural runoff

4   Allowance for ecosystem restoration

5   No use of pesticides, herbicides, or fertilizers

6   Use of seventy to ninety percent less water

7   Greatly reduced food miles

8   More control of food safety and security

9   New employment opportunities

10 Purification of grey water to drinking water

11 Animal feed from postharvest plant material

In its most complete configuration, the vertical farm will consist of a complex of buildings constructed in close proximity to one another. They will include a building for growing; offices for management; a separate control center for monitoring the overall running of the facility; a nursery for selecting and germinating seeds; a quality-control laboratory to monitor food safety, document the nutritional status of each crop, and monitor for plant diseases; a building for the vertical farm workforce; an eco-education/tourist center for the general public; a green market; and eventually a restaurant.

What follows is based on the construction of an experimental prototype vertical farm. The farm itself would be modest in height, perhaps five stories tall and maybe an eighth of a city block in footprint (totaling one-and-a-quarter acres, and allowing over ten acres of farmland to return to its natural state). The interior space would be highly flexible, allowing the expert team of controlled indoor-agriculture scientists the maximum freedom to configure and reconfigure the conditions the crops will be subject to. They would work closely with local communities of consumers, a team of material scientists and structural engineers, and a state-of-the-art construction facility for the selection of crops and the custom manufacture of hydroponic and aeroponic equipment.

Once the construction of the vertical farm complex is complete, the selection of materials and seeds begins. Once selected and received, the seed must be surface decontaminated, then sent to the diagnostic laboratory for testing for the presence of microbial pathogens that might be commandeering them as their Trojan horse. Once certified disease-free, the seeds will be sent to the nursery for quality-control testing and germination. The nursery will be a separate facility from receiving, as the nursery is the first chance any pathogens might have of directly contaminating the inside of the vertical farm. The nursery and vertical farm will most likely be connected by a maximum-security pressurized lock system. The infant crops will be transferred to the vertical farm and situated into their hydroponic/aeroponic environment. All crops will be constantly monitored by remote sensing systems for growth and nutrient conditions. Much of the work in the nursery will be labor-intensive, creating many new job opportunities for those with a green thumb.

Water for the vertical farm will be used in hydroponic and aeroponic growing situations. The obvious advantage of controlled-environment agriculture is the fact that it is a "closed loop" system, thereby allowing for the capture of water vapor derived from the transpiration by employing dehumidification devices on each floor. This represents a highly efficient system of water use compared to the traditional mode of outdoor soil-based agricultural irrigation schemes. In the closed-loop system, hydroponics uses some seventy percent less water than conventional farming, while aeroponics uses seventy percent less water than hydroponics. Also, no runoff occurs in the vertical farm model. If implemented on a large scale, vertical farming would have the possibility of eliminating ocean pollution from agricultural runoff.

As for edible plants, one needs to consider several things before choosing which ones to grow. First, there are economic considerations. Is it worth the effort? Can farmers sell out the crop every time it's harvested, and at a profit? So far, a few popular vegetables have been grown successfully for profit. These include tomatoes, lettuce, spinach, zucchini, green peppers, and green beans. Hardly any of these crops would qualify for addressing the needs of a hungry world, however. Essential crops such as wheat, barley, millet, rice, and potatoes would be more appropriate. If their successful produce can now, within its own borders, supply its own population with an essential healthy diet, then profitability takes a backseat to need. Government sponsored food programs may become the determining economic factor in the form of incentives and the subsidies that enable the vertical farm to survive and even thrive, producing crops that in a free flowing market economy would ordinarily fail to generate enough income to make them worthwhile.

In order to set forth a mandate for repurposing the urban infrastructure, one must first have a clear picture of the characteristics that currently define any city. Once its features have been characterized, we can propose modifications to herald the new, sustainable city. Every municipality is unique in its physical configuration, geographic location, population composition, and system of governance. Yet each has in common the need to supply all of its citizens with essential services, most of which are either directly or indirectly dependent upon natural resources. Each activity—the supply of water, energy, and food—must be thoroughly examined with respect to whether it is currently sustainable. Next, those systems that comprise the functional substrate of the city (water mains, reservoirs, wastewater treatment/recycling facilities, communications systems, transportation infrastructure, to name a few), must be thoroughly delineated and quantified with respect to their actual resource footprint. Once these data are collated and synthesized, planners can begin the task of reconfiguring them into a cohesive, overarching plan of action.

In summary, the culmination of converting all major urban centers into eco-cities promises a healthier, longer, more productive life for each and every one of us, at least from an environmental perspective. The new city will carry out its mission with a deep respect for that part of the world that supplies it with its essential resources. The non-urban portion of the earth will not be able to flourish again until its most advanced life form realizes that an intact natural world is its most economical, sustainable, practical system of life support.

A portion of this essay is an edited excerpt from the book *The Vertical Farm: Feeding the World in the 21st Century*, published in 2010 by Macmillan.

Yuri Avvakumov's *House of Cards*

Michael Govan

As he was finishing his architecture studies in Moscow in the early 1980s, Yuri Avvakumov focused his practice almost entirely on drawings and models to be entered in architectural competitions. Freeing himself of the requirement to turn his ideas into physical buildings (which at that time in the Soviet Union would have been unlikely in any case) Avvakumov reconsidered the aspirations of early Soviet suprematist and constructivist architecture and developed a hybrid art/architecture practice he dubbed Paper Architecture.

The utopian spirit of the historical Russian avant-garde is perhaps best exemplified by Vladimir Tatlin's never-built proposal for a spiraling steel *Monument to the Third International* (1920), reminiscent of the Eiffel Tower, but intended for government use. Incorporating offices as well as radio broadcast facilities, the futuristic tower embraced the technological age in what the artist described as "a union of purely artistic forms for a utilitarian purpose." Today, Tatlin's revolutionary ambitions for architecture—preserved only in a few ghostly black-and-white photographs of his model—are considered romantic, if not tragic. After spending his last years in a failed effort to build a personal glider, Tatlin died, unrecognized, as an artistic Icarus: symbolic of the failure of his and his compatriots' high-flying hopes for art and architecture to transform society and government.

Avvakumov's "houses of cards" are made on the scale of toys, yet with the precision of an engineer. They are as linguistically playful as they are critically incisive. The feat of stacking playing cards into a fragile mock-architecture based solely on friction and balance is a centuries-old tradition. Avvakumov's witty structures can, ironically, be repeatedly erected and collapsed as they are stitched together with tape, thread, or rubber bands. Perhaps a playful reference to the last years of the Soviet state—a fragile "house of cards" somehow glued together and rising up in repeated displays of power—the artist's phallic skyscraper-like constructions, however, resonate with ever present questions about the aims of art and technology expressed in architecture.

Avvakumov is fascinated by the role of towers, and has, with ambivalence, occasionally built his own functional structures. Recently, for an exhibition of paintings by contemporary artists staged in a huge hangar-like gallery, he created a mini city of several tall pavilions made of cargo storage racks. Shifting the usual vantage point for paintings to a higher plane, he remarked: "I had in mind a town center, complete with a tower they could climb for a better view."

In the end Avvakumov proposes no ideological or political position. Utilizing the subtle critical mechanisms of irony, humor, and engineering, his work engenders a critical consciousness about our human ambition for reaching greater heights, in design, or in civilization.

Yuri Avvakumov. *Catapultower*, 1982 (reconstruction 2007), playing cards, height variable

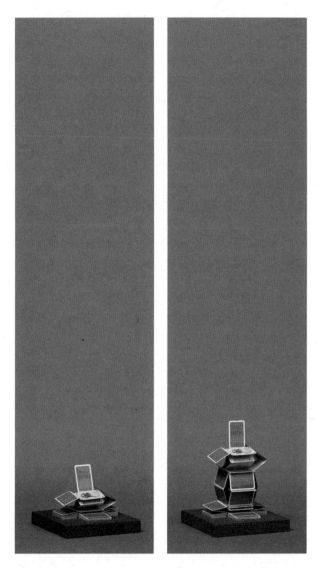

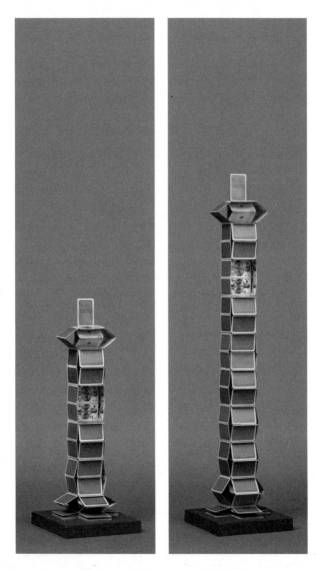

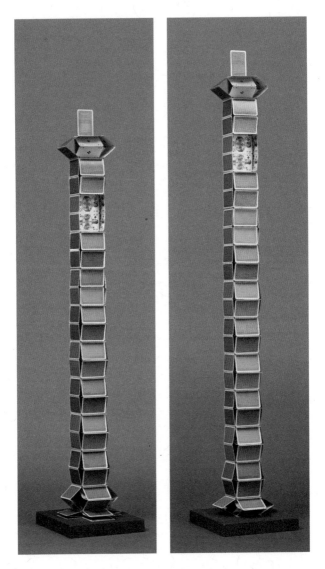

About the Contributors

Philip Nobel has written architecture criticism for *The New York Times*, *The Nation*, *Artforum*, and *Metropolis* among many other publications. His book on the reconstruction of the World Trade Center site—*Sixteen Acres: Architecture and the Outrageous Struggle for the Future of Ground Zero*—was published in 2005. That same year, he co-founded the short-lived, but influential, architecture gossip blog *The Gutter*. Nobel received his M.Arch degree from Columbia University in 1995.

Bruce Sterling—futurist, journalist, science-fiction author, design critic—is best known for his novels and his seminal work on the *Mirrorshades* anthology, which defined the cyberpunk genre. His nonfiction works include *The Hacker Crackdown: Law and Disorder on the Electronic Frontier*; *Tomorrow Now: Envisioning the Next Fifty Years*; and *Shaping Things*. He is a contributing editor of *Wired* magazine and has appeared in *Time*, *The Wall Street Journal*, *The New York Times*, *Metropolis*, and many other venues.

Tom Vanderbilt is the author of *Traffic: Why We Drive the Way We Do (and What It Says About Us)* and *Survival City: Adventures Among the Ruins of Atomic America*. He is contributing editor for *Wired UK*, *Outside*, and *Artforum*, and has written for many publications, ranging from *The New York Times* to *Smithsonian* to *Cabinet*. He lives in Brooklyn, NY.

Matthew Yglesias is a prominent writer on public policy and economics, and the author of *The Rent Is Too Damn High*. He has been based variously at *The American Prospect*, *The Atlantic*, and most-recently at *Slate*, before leaving in February 2014 to join Vox Media. He lives in Washington.

Diana Lind is the Director of Digital Audience Development for Philadelphia Media Network, a company that includes *The Philadelphia Inquirer*, *Daily News*, and Philly.com. Prior to that, she was Executive Director and Editor in Chief of the urban affairs website, *Next City*. She is the author of *Brooklyn Modern* (Rizzoli, 2008) and has been a frequent contributor to *Architectural Record*.

Will Self is the author of ten novels, six collections of shorter fiction, and six of non-fiction. He is a pro-lific journalist and a prominent broadcaster in the UK, and is also Professor of Contemporary Thought at Brunel University. He lives in London.

Emily Badger is a writer in Washington, where she covers national urban policy for *The Washington Post*. She writes frequently about urban planning, housing, transportation, poverty, and inequality—and why we can't talk about any of these topics without mentioning the others as well.

Dickson Despommier is a professor in the Department of Environmental Health Sciences at Columbia University's Mailman School of Public Health. He is also the director of the Vertical Farm Project, which addresses issues related to urban agriculture, environmental disturbance, and the restoration of damaged ecosystems. The project was started in 1999 as a classroom activity in Dr. Despommier's Medical Ecology course.

Michael Govan was president and director of Dia Art Foundation in New York City from 1994 to 2006. In 2006 he joined the Los Angeles County Museum of Art (LACMA) as Director.

Acknowledgments

We would like to thank the following for their support in the creation and completion of this volume of SOM Thinkers: Carolina Burdo, Olin McKenzie, Colin Koop, Diana Murphy, Jud Ehrbar, Claire Nau, Thomas de Monchaux, Nicholas Adams, Eugenia Bell, John Fawcett, Adam Heimlich, Katie George, and Jacqueline Thaw.

Editor: Philip Nobel
Managing editor: Amy Gill
Project director for Metropolis Books: Diana Murphy
Copyediting: Eugenia Bell
Graphic design: Neil Donnelly and Sean Yendrys
Printing: Oliver Printing Co., Twinsburg, Ohio, USA

This book is set in Concorde and Plain, and printed on
Rolland Enviro 100 Smooth Text and Cover

Library of Congress Cataloging-in-Publication Data is
available upon request.

ISBN 978-1-938922-78-7

Metropolis Books
ARTBOOK | D.A.P.
155 Sixth Avenue, 2nd fl.
New York, NY 10013
T: 212 627 1999 x 213
F: 212 627 9484
www.artbook.com

FSC
www.fsc.org
RECYCLED
Paper made from
recycled material
FSC® C002614